PUBLISHED BY
DEBBIE MITCHELL PUBLICATIONS
304 W. CHERYL
HURST, TX 76053
1-800-282-2836
1-817-282-6890 (Phone or Fax)

❤ ❤ ❤

GRAPHIC DESIGN BY
PAT MC CLURE, C.C. PUBLICATIONS
665 TIMBER RD.
HARLAN, IA 51537

PHOTOGRAPHY BY
HARRIG PHOTO DESIGN
3316 SO. 66TH AVE.
OMAHA, NE 68106

❤ ❤ ❤

PRINTING BY
TRAFTON PRINTING, INC.
109 S. FILLMORE, P.O. BOX 9068
AMARILLO, TX 79105

❤ ❤ ❤ **SUPPLY SOURCES** ❤ ❤ ❤

Most all of my wood designs are my own creations. All wood projects and some of the other project supplies may be purchased directly though Debbie Mitchell Publications, 304 W. Cheryl, Hurst, TX 76053, (800) 282-2836 or (817) 282-6890 (phone or fax). A few purchased wood items have the sources listed in the individual projects and they may be contacted directly if preferred. Whenever possible, I have listed the sources for the extra decorating supplies used. Check your local craft stores for all kinds of decorating notions, paints, and supplies, etc.

SUPPLIES

PAINTS
DELTA CERAMCOAT
Black
Black Green
Bright Yellow
Brown Iron Oxide
Burnt Sienna
Cayenne
Crocus
Empire Gold
Flesh Tan
Hammered Iron
Hunter Green
Ivory
Light Ivory

Maple Sugar Tan
Midnight Blue
Mocha Brown
Mudstone
Old Parchment
Pumpkin
Sandstone
Seminole Green
Spice Tan
Sunbright Yellow
Territorial Beige
Trail Tan
Yellow

DELTA CERAMCOAT GLEAMS
Kim Gold
Pearl Finish
DELTA RENAISSANCE FOIL
Adhesive
Burnished Silver
Holiday Colors (red and green)
DECOART AMERICANA
Dark Pine
Forest Green
Leaf Green
Mistletoe
Santa Red
Ultra Blue Deep
White Wash

DECOART TRUE COLORS
Blue Violet
DECOART HEAVENLY HUES
Glitter
DECOART DIMENSIONS
Green Iridescent
White Iridescent
OR
PLAID ENTERPRISES FASHION SHOW DIMENSIONAL PAINT
Pearl Champagne
Pearl White
Shiny Bright Green
LIQUITEX TUBE ACRYLIC ARTIST COLORS
Burnt Umber
ACCENT COUNTRY COLORS
Pineneedle Green
Raw Sienna
JO SONJA'S ARTISTS' COLORS
Napthol Red Light

MEDIUMS, FINISHES, AND SEALERS
DecoArt Snow-Tex Textural Medium
Delta Ceramcoat Textile Medium
Designs From The Heart Wood Sealer
FolkArt Extender (Plaid)
J.W. Etc. Right-Step Water Base Varnish, Matte, Satin, or Gloss
J.W.Etc. First-Step Wood Sealer

BRUSHES

LOEW-CORNELL
Series #7300 Flat: #1, #2, #4, #6, #8. #10, #12
Series 7350 Liner: #00, #1, #4
OR
ROYAL BRUSHES
Golden Taklon Series #700 Flat: 3/4"
Golden Taklon Series #150 Flat: #1, #2, #4, #6, #8, #12
Golden Taklon Series #250 Liner: #1
Royal Garden Series #R8595: #5/0
OTHER BRUSHES
Old "Scruffy" flat brushes in a variety of sizes ranging from #2 through #10 (used for Stippling Fur Technique)
Variety of fabric brushes (flats and liner)

GENERAL SUPPLIES

Cotton swabs
Creative Paperclay (1/2 lb. or 1/4 lb. pkg.)
Disposable palette (for acrylics)
Emery boards
Glue (Mighty Tacky Glue or Strong Epoxy and hot glue gun)
Graphite paper, black and white
Grey pastel chalk pencil
Kneaded eraser
Lint-free cloths or sponge brushes to apply sealer
MICRON Pigma Waterproof Pen, #01 fine width
Model Magic Modeling Compound (Binney & Smith, Inc.)
Natural sea sponge (fine/pores)
Nylon fishing line
Old toothbrush (for spattering)
Palette knife (Loew-Cornell J-0 Series)
Paper towels
Pencils
Ruler or scale (straight edge)
Sandpaper, medium and fine grit
Sculpting tool set and clay shaper tool (optional)
Stylus
Tack cloth
Tracing paper
Water basin
Wire cutters
X-Acto knife and single edge razor blade

OTHER SUPPLIES

"Dress It Up" &
Co.,
20 gauge gold
#32029-4)
ALL COOPED UP DESIGNS STRINGLETS (String Doll Hair NATURAL)
Curling ribbon, red and green colors
Embroidery thread, navy blue, green, red, and ivory (optional)
Eye screws, tiny gold colored
Fabric strips of dotted material, red, green, navy, etc.
Fabric strips of gingham check, red/black, red/white, green/black, green/white, green/beige, and blue/black
Fabric strips of plaid, red, green, and navy
Iridescent cellophane tissue, small piece to wrap candy
Jingle bells, 6mm, 9mm, and 15mm gold, 6mm and 10mm red
Lace, ivory color, 1 1/2" width and 3" width
Metallic gold tie cording to hang ornaments, to border cheese box lid, and to use in a few embellishments of ornaments (2 sizes used - fine and medium)
Miniature green garland
Miniature icicle garland with 3/4" - 1/2" length icicles
Miniature poinsettia/holly silk flowers
Natural jute string
Pin backings, 3/4" length
S'getti String, green (1" length is all that's needed)
Satin crepe ribbon, red, 1/2" or 3/4" width for sash and obi on Panda Bear
Satin ribbon, off white, red, and green in 1/16", 1/8", and 1/4" widths
Satin ribbon, royal blue 1/2" and 1/16" width
Satin ribbon, yellow 1/16" width
Stencil for checks (Source: Those Little Details, "Checks, Hearts, Stars, and Stripes", purchased from Sharon And Gayle Publications, SGP 1001, P.O. Box 16394, Covington, KY 41015)
Suede leather scrap pieces, brown and red
Thread, heavy-duty white or ivory (used to string paperclay beads and gathering lace for pins and tree topper, etc.)
White Doll Hair/Trims (Source: "Velvet Stream" Fleece & Unicorn Doll Hair Co., Rt. 5, Box 368, Stillwater, OK 74074)
Wire of your choice, 19 gauge or double-braided twisted wire used for halos and heavy, stronger wire used on spiral to hold up Tree Topper
NOTE: Items such as bells, ribbons, cording and any other similar items is listed in the individual project instructions.

TERMS, TECHNIQUES, AND PRODUCTS

WOOD PREPARATION

Fill any holes with wood filler and sand. Sand all pieces in the direction of the wood grain. Wipe clean with a tack cloth or lint free rag. I use Designs From The Heart Wood Sealer for a fast drying sealer. There are plenty of other sealers that are widely used. Choose your favorite. After the sealer has dried completely, lightly sand again. At this point, the pieces are ready to apply patterns and basecoat. Proper wood preparation is important for the final outcome of your finished piece.

(CONTINUED ON PAGE 6)

TRANSFERRING THE PATTERN

The outcome of your painted project can be determined by the care and accuracy of your tracing of the pattern. Trace your design onto a sheet of tracing paper first. Use either a well sharpened pencil or a fine point black marker pen. This tracing will be used to transfer the pattern onto your wood piece. Having the pattern on tracing paper enables you to see through to line up on your wood piece. There are several ways to transfer the pattern. I have two favorite ways, depending on the color of the basecoat. One is to re-trace the backside of the tracing paper pattern using a grey pastel chalk pencil or to use a regular pencil lead and do the same. Once the pattern is turned right side up and lined up on the wood piece, then use a stylus to transfer. The chalk or pencil lead will take the place of graphite paper and will act as carbon to transfer the pattern to the wood. You may prefer to use a piece of graphite paper to slide between the pattern and the wood piece. Use an old piece of graphite if possible or wipe new graphite with a paper towel on the carbon side before using. Whatever transferring method is used, be sure to use a light touch and not bear down too hard. It is best to let your basecoats dry completely before transferring the pattern. If the tracing lines should become too dark and bold, use your kneaded eraser to buff down and lighten the lines. The kneaded eraser will lighten but not smear or make eraser marks. Trace only the lines that are necessary, leaving off small details such as eyelashes and high-light dots, stripes, prints and plaids in clothing, and comma strokes. To indicate a comma stroke, place a line in the center of a stroke area. Remember also, that certain portions of the patterns may be applied first, then basecoated. After ample drying time, more pattern sections or details will be applied

BASECOATS

You may be required to basecoat a surface completely with one color, then dry, and re-apply pattern portions to basecoat additional areas of the design. Then again, you may have projects which require that you apply the pattern for major basecoated areas first. Basecoat accordingly, and when dried completely, the detail lines of the patterns are re-traced. The individual project instructions will list the color used to basecoat the various areas of each design. When basecoating the wood pieces, be sure to continue the color and pattern around the edges of the pieces using the appropriate colors. Keep in mind that your basecoating will also determine the final appearance of the finished project. Basecoats can be applied with either a flat brush or a sponge brush when basecoating larger pieces. Do not use a round or liner brush. This will leave a built-up ridge of paint and not a smooth surface. It is important to have both a smooth surface and solid coverage. Most paints will require at least two or more coats. Paint in one direction whenever possible. Let each coat dry completely before applying the second coat.

WASH

This term refers to a wash of stain using Burnt Umber in some projects. This is done by thinning the Burnt Umber with water to achieve a transparent color. This is used to paint a stain effect. It is better to have a light stain to start with and add more color to deepen than have it too dark. It will be important not to get too deep in color so that your sideload floated shading will define the details.

SIDELOAD FLOAT

Use a large flat brush, when possible, to float color. Occasionally I'll use the small flats for the smaller detail areas. Sideload floated color may be referred to throughout the instructions as a sideload or just floated color. I normally use a sideload float for the shaded areas, using the shade colors listed. In some cases I may float highlights, especially to strengthen them. Each project will have highlight and shade colors listed for each pattern section. To accomplish the sideload float technique, first dip a flat brush into water and lightly lay each side of the brush on a folded paper towel to blot the brush slightly. Do not press too firmly on the towel or you will dry out the brush too much. An over abundance of water in the brush will cause the paint to flow across the brush completely, leaving a faint, "washy" stripe of color on your painting. Too little water will result in a stronger, "draggy" dry brush effect. The object is to have just the right amount of water in your brush so that you will have color on one side of the brush, fading out to water on the opposite side. After dampening the brush with water, dip one corner into your color. Place the brush on your palette and bear down to blend using a sweeping motion in the same spot. This should allow the paint on the one side to start to fade lighter towards the water side of the brush.

SHADING

Using the darker shade colors listed in each individual section of each design, sideload float.

DOUBLELOADED HIGHLIGHTS

I double load my highlight colors most of the time. Once basecoating is complete and the detail pattern is re-applied. I then proceed to load a flat brush about 1/2 to 3/4 into the base color. The opposite side is tipped into the highlight color listed for that particular section. With the two colors on the brush, firmly apply pressure to the brush and blend on the palette. Stay in one small area and brush in a sweeping motion. Flip the brush over to the other side and repeat the blending process. This will blend the colors on both sides of the brush. The key is to load the brush with plenty of paint and blend in one small area on the palette. This will tone down the highlight color to achieve a gradual change from the base color to highlight color. Do not use water for this technique. Be sure to pick up lots of paint on the brush to have a creamy blend. After the highlights are complete, I apply any fabric print on the clothing designs, then shade with a sideload float of the shade color.

DRY BRUSHING

It may be easier to actually use a "dry", flat brush to start with. (Preferably an older brush and not a brand new one.) This technique can prove to be hard on brushes. Tip the end of the brush into your paint. Brush a few strokes onto your palette to remove some of the excess paint. In some instances you may also brush across a dry paper towel. Then, with a light stroke, brush against your painting surface. The look you want to achieve is a dry, gritty, grainy, light, draggy appearance. In most instances, I like to brush across the surface in an up and down motion, then back and forth, left to right.

SPATTERING

This procedure is done with an old toothbrush. Place the color you plan to spatter with on a palette or in an appropriate container. Dip a toothbrush into water, then into the paint. Mix well. This should be "India ink" consistency. If too much water is added, the paint will become too transparent. Enough pigment is needed to prevent it from being washed out. After loading the toothbrush,

blot well with paper towels. Aim the bristles toward the project to be spattered. Using your thumb, flick the bristles while moving constantly, to spatter evenly.

LINERWORK

Using a liner brush, thin paint to an ink consistency. To load the liner brush, pull through the paint, twisting the brush as you pull to make a fine point. Using a light touch on the tip of the brush will keep the lines thin. The heavier that pressure is applied, the thicker the lines will become.

PAINTING PLAIDS AND CHECKS

When faced with the task of any of the following instructions, don't panic. It is easier than it looks. One important point is that the paint consistency should be VERY TRANSPARENT in color. If the color is too strong, when the strokes cross over each other, there will be no contrast for that intersecting check. If there is no contrast, the plaid and checked look is lost. I always strengthen that intersecting check for a more prominent square. This is what probably takes the most time. Another thing to watch is your placement of stripes. Paint each section of clothing separately. Follow the contour lines of that particular section, creating a slight curvature to each line or stripe placed. This will look more natural than striping everything straight up and down and straight across. When applying stripes for use in miniature gingham checks, plaids, and ticking, I use a #1 liner brush in small areas. This is done with a very transparent color also. Keep in mind, that when using a liner brush, you need to flatten the bristles for a wider stripe. Load the brush with color and work back and forth in a sweeping motion to flatten the bristles. A common mistake is to not only have the paint consistency too dark in color, but not applying enough pressure to allow the bristles to flatten. If the liner brush is used without flattening, the lining will look like any other normal thin liner work or stripes. After all details for plaids and checks have been applied, shade all creases, folds, and any major pattern lines. Shading will seem to bring everything together at this point. Like most projects I design and paint, the techniques are not so difficult when broken down step-by-step. It just involves time and patience. Another hint to keep in mind is that if you start spacing any of these designs close together, it's obvious there will be more detail work involved. The further apart each design is placed, will mean less work!

TIPS FOR STRIPING PEPPERMINT CANDY STICKS

To paint a dowel stick to look like a peppermint candy cane, basecoat first with White Wash. To achieve an even, spiral stripe around the stick, use a piece of curling ribbon (the kind used for wrapping packages) or tiny 1/16" to 1/8" wide satin ribbon and attach with tape to one end of the dowel. Wrap the ribbon around the dowel as close as you want the stripes to be, then tape the other end in place. Use a pencil to mark each side of the ribbon, remove, and you have a pattern for the stripe. Basecoat with the desired colors as I have done on a couple of the projects. This usually results in a pretty good lookin' candy cane!

WOODEN CUTOUTS

I do want you to be aware that some of the ornaments are dimensional with extra cutouts attached and the same applies to other projects in this book. Remaining dimension has been achieved with the use of Snow-Tex and Paperclay or Model Magic. All ornaments are now hung by using the tiny gold colored eye screws (when using 1/4" thick wood cutouts) and the gold metallic tie cording. SPECIAL NOTE: All ornaments are finished on the back with a solid coat of Black Green.

SNOW-TEX

I have tried to think of many ways to use various mediums in my projects whenever possible. I've especially enjoyed the many uses that I have found with DecoArt Snow-Tex Textural Medium. In a couple of projects found in this book, I have managed to give texture as well as a raised three dimensional look in the gingerbread cookies and candy treats. When using Snow-Tex, you can achieve a puffy, smoother look by using a palette knife. I prefer a small, narrow tipped, flexible knife. Scoop up a generous amount of Snow-Tex and pat into place on your wood surface to be sure that it adheres to the surface well. Keep adding more Snow-Tex and gradually push it to the edge of the design or cut edge of the wood piece. With a light patting motion using the palette knife, the Snow-Tex will stay built up and rather smooth. It seems to let the moisture rise to the top and the gritty ingredient stays just under the surface. If you choose to achieve a more gritty look, apply a thinner coat with the palette knife or an old brush. Dry thoroughly, then paint. Snow-Tex can be mixed with paint, then applied to the surface, or painted with a transparent wash directly on top. I have preferred to apply Snow-Tex first, dry completely, then paint with transparent washes. This way stronger color can be applied to the shaded areas, yet this lets more Snow-Tex show through in the highlight areas. Snow-Tex may be applied on top of Paperclay items also. Let dry, then paint.

CREATIVE PAPERCLAY AND MODEL MAGIC

This is a sculpting medium that air dries without baking and is relatively light in weight. To hasten drying time it is possible to place it in an oven at 200 degrees for 10-15 minutes or use a hair dryer. When air drying, a drying rack of some sort would be very beneficial to allow air to circulate on all sides. This will be helpful to dry more evenly throughout. Take out only the amount you need to work with at the time. Keep the remaining Paperclay in an airtight container or zip-lock bag to keep it from drying out. I do keep a moist piece of sponge or paper towel inside the container for additional moisture. Paperclay can be used entirely on it's own or can adhere to a wood cutout surface. Most pieces in this publication have the clay adhered to the wood pieces. The Paperclay has been used in a manner to give dimension to the designs which captures a more realistic quality to the projects. A variety of uses includes tiny buttons, cookies, candies, and paws, ears, and muzzles on some of the bears. Be creative and give any of your painting pieces dimension! For more ideas and technique usage with the Paperclay refer to other projects shown in my "Cozy Cubby Companion" and "We're Back..." editions also.

Keep Paperclay moistened while working and kneading, by wiping your hands across a wet paper towel or sponge. Dipping your fingers directly into water may result in too much moisture, causing the clay to be wet, tacky, and uncontrollable. If it does become uncontrollable, add more Paperclay to soak up the moisture and allow you to work it again. It is important to use water, either on a brush or your finger, to moisten the Paperclay to mend, to join pieces together, and to smooth out any cracks, wrinkles, or bumps to achieve a smooth surface. Moistening your wood piece with a small amount of water before applying the Paperclay will help to adhere the clay to the wood. You may use glue to help reinforce this if needed. To give the look that the molded Paperclay formations are part of the wood and not have a definite seam line to look as if it was glued on, work with your fingers, tools, and brush, to blend and smear part of the clay tightly against the wood. Clean up the messy residue by using brushes or cotton swabs that have been moistened with water and working from the outer residue edge back towards the dimensional Paperclay piece. This will clean your wood and seal the Paperclay against it as well. Any holes or grooves are to be done before the Paperclay has dried using a piece of wire, a stylus, a toothpick, etc. Dry completely. To smooth the surface even more, use an emery board or a piece of fine grit sandpaper and lightly sand before painting.

In this book of projects I have chosen to use Model Magic Modeling Compound occasionally, rather than Creative Paperclay. When forming tiny small items such as buttons, round peppermint candies and the tiny square letter blocks, the Model Magic tends to form more smoothly and leaves no cracks along the outer edges that have to be worked with to smooth out as is necessary when using the Paperclay. Pinch off the very smallest amounts as well as larger pieces to get the desired size needed for the particular project. Roll into a smooth ball, then flatten to the diameter size required. Next, use something to indent the inner portion of your disc. This will give the look of small buttons with a rim on the outer edges. Poke holes if desired in the center. Dry, paint, and glue into place.

GLIMMER CLEAR AND HEAVENLY HUES GLITTER

DecoArt Heavy Metals, Glimmer Clear is used for the final sugar sparkle on the candy pieces. This will remain tacky to the touch and not ever dry completely. This will however, go away once the piece is varnished. A newer product to try for this procedure is the Heavenly Hues Glitter. It leaves no tacky sticky finish.

FOLKART EXTENDER

There are several uses for this medium. In the projects for this book I used it to help with highlighting and shading some of the candies. The most important thing I want to point out is how to apply the extender, then shade or highlight. First, apply extender to the project surface with a flat brush, working it well until it has a "satiny" film. Be careful not to use too much. Do not leave puddles on your painting surface. Brush back and forth one direction, then the other, working it well into the surface. Sideload your brush, blend on the palette, and apply color where needed. Now, quickly use a soft, dry, fluffy brush to lightly buff and soften the color towards the outer edges. You want a fading effect. The soft fluffy brush can be a mop brush, or just a dry, flat brush. Use a very soft touch to the surface when buffing colors. Remember, too much extender will result in moving a wash of color around. It is very important to have just a light film on the surface so that it appears "satiny." Another important tip is to cover the entire area and beyond with extender so that you can move the color well and let it fade out. If you should stop too short of an area, your color will grab and bluntly stop at that point, rather than soften into the original base color.

GENERAL BEAR INSTRUCTIONS

The bears in each project in this book will be done in the same colors and stippling technique. COMPLETELY read the instructions given for the step-by-step process for the fur technique. As you proceed, refer to your printed pattern and the color photos for shading and highlight placement.

I prefer a different approach when painting my furry characters. It may seem to some to be a little backwards, but, ...what can I say! After countless hours of doing my fur technique, I can probably do it in my sleep. I choose to complete my bears' fur and faces before dressing them. This gives me the feeling of accomplishment. Each bear then has personality and is ready for it's clothing. I then re-stipple over the edges where any fur meets an article of clothing or another object after the total completion of either of those necessary pattern articles. Some feel more comfortable doing just the opposite and finishing all clothing first, then completing the character with the fur. Either way is correct. The main thing is to enjoy what you do.

PALETTE
DELTA CERAMCOAT
Black
Ivory
Maple Sugar Tan
Old Parchment
Spice Tan
DECOART AMERICANA
White Wash
LIQUITEX TUBE ACRYLIC ARTIST COLORS
Burnt Umber
ACCENT COUNTRY COLORS
Raw Sienna
JO SONJA'S ARTISTS' COLORS
Napthol Red Light

OTHER SUPPLIES
FolkArt Extender

BASECOAT AND SHADE

Basecoat the body sections with Spice Tan. Apply the pattern for the features and details. Sideload float the shaded areas on the fur with Raw Sienna. Follow the pattern for the correct placement for shading around all features. Shading is represented on patterns by tiny cluster dots. Shade along the correct sides of lines, behind some areas to allow other areas to stand out. If shaded on the wrong side, it will cover areas to be highlighted.

STIPPLING

I use old worn brushes for this technique. Some painters prefer to use a deerfoot brush. Pounce the brush on your palette to fray or spread the bristles further apart. Do not use water in the brush. Dip the end of the entire brush into paint and pounce on the palette with an up-and-down motion to remove the excess paint so that you can achieve a light, airy effect. When stippling the fur area on your project, lightly use the same up-and-down motion. Overlap this light stipple and keep moving the brush to cover the entire fur area with a light, airy look. Be careful not to pounce hard and smash the color in. Don't skip from place to place as this will cause a splotchy polka dotted effect.

One major point to remember through the next few steps is to GRADUALLY work through the highlight colors from the darkest to the lightest. Do not go too light too fast!

BEAR FUR HIGHLIGHT COLOR COMBINATIONS TO BE USED IN ORDER
1. Spice Tan + Maple Sugar Tan
2. Maple Sugar Tan
3. Maple Sugar Tan + Old Parchment
4. Old Parchment
5. Old Parchment + Ivory
6. Ivory

STEP 1

Load the stippling brush into a mixture of the base color, Spice Tan, and Maple Sugar Tan. This color should be slightly lighter than your basecoat color. If you were to stipple Maple Sugar Tan alone, it would be too bright and strong, not just a subtle change. Keep in mind that as paint dries it appears darker. You may need to add more Maple Sugar Tan to your mix if it doesn't show up. Stipple over the entire fur areas including the shaded areas. Keep it light and airy! Be careful not to pounce hard so you can avoid splotchy spots that will eventually basecoat that area.

STEP 2

Always keep the above color combination in your brush THROUGHOUT THE NEXT FEW HIGHLIGHTING STEPS. Occasionally, the brush will tend to collect dried balls of paint on the flared bristles. Rinse and dry it with paper towels, then re-load. With the original mix in your brush, tip one side into Maple Sugar Tan. Pounce on the palette to blend. The Maple Sugar Tan side of this brush will be a stronger highlight along the highlighted areas. To avoid a striped highlight line around the outer edge, start lightly walking your highlight back towards the center of each section. As you approach the center, just touch slightly here and there. This will show a hint of all of the highlight colors throughout all of the fur areas and not just at the outer edges. This should give more dimension and a more rounded look to the bear.

STEP 3

The next highlight color is Maple Sugar Tan + Old Parchment. Repeat the stronger highlight in the same highlighted areas walking back towards the center also.

STEP 4

This step will use Old Parchment alone. From this step on, don't apply the highlight as heavily and do not walk the color towards the center as much. Simply highlight certain areas.

STEP 5

The next highlight color is Old Parchment + Ivory. Just a slight touch will be needed.

STEP 6

The last highlight color is Ivory. Use it only if needed. (Usually on the muzzle/cheek areas, etc.)

STEP 7

Now that the initial stippling is complete, sideload float using Raw Sienna in all of the shaded areas again. Use FolkArt Extender instead of water for floating the color. This should remain light in color so that there will not be a dark, harsh edge. You will notice that by using a light colored float, the fur will show through. Just a little bit will make a big difference. Use a larger flat brush so that this shading will work through the body rather than develop a build-up of color on the edges of the fur areas. Keep in mind that the original shading lies underneath. The object is to lightly bring this shading back up to the surface where it may have been lost until now.

STEP 8

After the Raw Sienna shading is dry, strengthen the areas that need to be darkened using Burnt Umber. Sideload float using water with your paint this time. This shading is usually located around the facial features such as the eyes, muzzles, mouths, ears, and anywhere else that might need emphasizing.

STEP 9

Basecoat the eyes and noses with Black. Highlight with a sideload of White Wash.

STEP 10

Using a #2 flat brush and a sideload float of Burnt Umber, touch slightly elongated C-strokes for whisker marks on the sides of the muzzles. At this point add more highlights or shading if needed before adding cheek color.

STEP 11

Cheek color is applied by brushing FolkArt Extender back and forth, then up and down, repeatedly, over the entire surface of the muzzle, until a "satin film" has been achieved. Avoid a dripping wet puddled coverage. If it is too wet, the cheek color will bleed and run uncontrollably and make it impossible to buff and soften the color properly. Use a dry, fluffy flat brush or a mop brush to very slightly buff Napthol Red Light onto the cheek areas to fade it into the muzzle. You can touch a bit of color to the lip area if desired.

A FINAL NOTE

If more instruction and visual guidance is required for this particular fur technique, refer to my "Keep On Stipplin'" book for a more detailed, full color, step-by-step procedure from start to finish. It also demonstrates most commonly made mistakes that are done incorrectly and shows the correct look to achieve.

COZY CUBBY COUSINS

I am introducing the "Cozy Cubby Cousins" for their debut appearance. It is inspiration from all of our international painting friends that has prompted me to design the Koala Cousin, Panda Cousin, and Polar Bear Cousin to unite all the Cubbies in a truly unique combination for decorating your Christmas tree. They still take on the "Cubby" look, as well as being individuals themselves.

KOALA COUSIN
COLOR PHOTO ON PAGE 4

PALETTE
DELTA CERAMCOAT
Black
Dark Chocolate
Flesh Tan
Hammered Iron
Ivory
Lt. Ivory
Mocha Brown
Mudstone
Trail Tan
DECOART AMERICANA
Mistletoe
White Wash
DECOART HEAVENLY HUES
Glitter
JO SONJA'S ARTISTS' COLORS
Napthol Red Light
LIQUITEX TUBE ACRYLIC ARTIST COLORS
Burnt Umber

OTHER SUPPLIES
4 red jingle bells, 10mm or 15mm
Creative Paperclay
FolkArt Extender
Metallic told tie cording, fine and medium
Needle and thread or sewing machine
Snow-Tex Textural Medium
Suede leather scrap pieces in red and brown colors
Tacky Glue
Tiny gold eye screw

PREPARATION
   Sand, seal, and sand again. Apply pattern for all basic design areas to be basecoated. (Re-apply pattern after basecoating is complete to define all features, body sections, creases, and folds, etc.)

PAINTING PROCEDURE
1. BEAR FUR: Refer to the General Bear Instructions to familiarize yourself with the basic technique. This Koala bear will have a different palette of colors used in the layering of the fur, but will leave the same effect. Basecoat the body with Mudstone. Shade with Hammered Iron. Begin stippling using a mix of Mudstone and Trail Tan over the entire body. With this mix on your brush, load one end into Trail Tan, then begin the highlight steps. Next, use a combination of Trail Tan + Flesh Tan on the highlight side of the brush. Then use Flesh Tan alone, Flesh Tan + Ivory, Ivory alone, and finally

Ivory + Lt. Ivory. There is longer hair on the ears, along the back of the arm, on the back thigh, and on the heel to the bottom of the foot. Also, place a small amount on the back of the tail and surrounding each eye. Use a liner brush and gradually work from the highlight mix colors, working with the darker colors first, gradually pulling into lighter colors. Trail Tan, Flesh Tan, Ivory, then Lt. Ivory are the colors used in sequence. As you begin with the darker shades of colors your strokes with be fairly plenty. As you build into the lighter combinations, the strokes should become fewer, to prevent having too much coverage that will run the risk of losing layers of hair. Use extender on the brush constantly. This will allow the paint to flow easier and create a wispy look like real hair. You want to have a finished look of more Lt. Ivory coloring. The final shading is done with a combination of Hammered Iron and a touch of Burnt Umber. The eyes and nose are basecoated with Dark Chocolate and highlighted with a doubleload of Dark Chocolate and Trail Tan. Shade with a sideload float of Black. The final highlight dots are White Wash. To blush the cheeks, brush on extender to create a soft satin film of moisture, tip into Napthol Red Light and place on the upper cheek areas. Immediately buff to soften the color using a mop brush or a dry, flat brush.

2. HAT (AKUBRA) AND VEST: Basecoat with Brown Iron Oxide and doubleload highlight with Brown Iron Oxide and Mocha Brown. Shade with a sideload float of Burnt Umber. The hat band is Napthol Red Light.

3. BOOMERANG: Lightly stain using a wash of Burnt Umber. The "Merry Christmas" lettering is painted with a liner brush using Napthol Red Light. Trim the lettering with a liner brush using Mistletoe.

4. CANDIES THAT ARE INSIDE BACK POUCH (DILLY BAG): All these candies are formed from Creative Paperclay. I made four candy canes, all painted in different color combinations. There are two peppermint discs and one gumdrop. (Refer to the Terms And Techniques section for more information on using Creative Paperclay and Model Magic. Pinch off a piece of clay and roll into a smooth ball. Lay onto the table and roll into small snake-line strand. Cut into four equal sections and bend over one end of each to form the hook curves for the candy canes. Pull off two equal amounts of clay and roll into smooth, rounded balls. Lay them on the table and use a piece of flat wood or something similar to press gently over the top, smashing or flattening to the desired thickness and diameter to form small miniature peppermint candies. Be sure to smooth the outer edges where they may have cracked! Form a small gumdrop in a similar way. There is a larger bottom

and a smaller top. Flatten on the bottom side and slightly on the top side. Dry. Apply a thin coat of Snow-Tex over the entire gumdrop for texture. When all candies are dried, basecoat everything except the green candy cane and gum-drop with White Wash. Basecoat one candy cane solid Mistletoe. Another candy cane is striped with Mistletoe large and thin stripes. One candy cane is alternated with Napthol Red Light and Mistletoe stripes and the last has large Napthol Red Light stripes with Mistletoe thin lines between. One of the peppermint candies has larger Mistletoe bands with small, thin Mistletoe lines between. The other mint has alternating Napthol Red Light and Mistletoe bands. Brush over the tops of all these candies with Heavenly Hues Glitter. With a wash brush loaded with water and Mistletoe, apply color to the gumdrop, leaving it transparent for highlight areas. Dry. Then sideload float with stronger Mistletoe to add deeper color in places. Stipple final highlights using White Wash along the upper edge mainly, then brush on Heavenly Hues Glitter for the sugar sparkle. Using these candies you will be filling the back pouch to give a more Christmas look to the ornament.

5. BACK POUCH AND BEDROLL (SWAG): I formed this by hand, stitching it together with a needle and thread. A machine would be much faster, I'm sure! Using a piece of scrap red suede leather, cut into a length about 2 1/2" long x 1 1/4" wide. Meet together and stitch with a very narrow seam. Cut a circle to fit the bottom diameter of the tube and stitch together to the inside. Slightly clip in a few places and turn to the right side. I stitched a loop of the thin gold metallic cording to the inside of the bag to secure and slip over the bear's head and hang to it's back. Fill the pouch with candies and glue inside. I also strapped a bedroll around the neck. It hangs loosely on the front side of the ornament. It is a strip of brown suede leather, rolled into a tight roll and tied off on each end with metallic gold cording. This strip is about 2 1/4" wide and only needs to be about 2" long, then rolled up tightly.

FINISH

Using green satin ribbon, thread into two of the red jingle bells after threading through the holes on the boomerang and tie into a bow. Repeat on the other end. (HINT: Put a drop of glue onto the knot of the bow and let dry. This will prevent the bow from coming untied.) Allow all glue to dry. Varnish.

PANDA COUSIN
COLOR PHOTO ON PAGE 4

PALETTE
DELTA CERAMCOAT
Black
DECOART AMERICANA
White Wash
DECOART HEAVENLY HUES
Glitter
JO SONJA'S ARTISTS' COLORS
Napthol Red Light

OTHER SUPPLIES
1/2" Or 3/4" wide red satin crepe ribbon
Creative Paperclay
FolkArt Extender
Metallic gold tie cording
Small piece of iridescent cellophane tissue
Small pieces of curling ribbons, red and green
Tacky Glue
Tiny gold eye screw
Tiny thin gold metallic string

PREPARATION
Sand, seal and sand again. Apply pattern for all basic design areas to be basecoated. (Re-apply pattern after the basecoating is completed to define all features, body sections, creases, folds, etc.)

PAINTING PROCEDURE
1. BEAR FUR: Refer to the General Bear Instructions to familiarize you with the basic technique. Although this Panda bear will have only two colors to work with for our stippled fur look and highlight areas, the idea will be the same. The color combinations are Black and White Wash. First, basecoat with Black and White Wash in the appropriate areas. Load an old, scruffy flat brush with Black and tip into a touch of White Wash. Pounce on the palette to blend the colors to a soft, medium grey color. Lightly stipple the black areas with this color. Load one side of the brush tip into a stronger bit of White Wash and blend before application. Start placing this color along the highlight areas. (Refer to the color photo and pattern for placement.) Gradually walk the highlight back into the body to let it fade out. Add more White Wash to the side of the brush tip to brighten the highlights. Be careful not to overdo this stippling as you may cover the black look completely! Come back with a sideload float of Black to re-define areas of creases and divisions of body sections. Shade the White Wash areas with a soft amount of Black. Using extender on your brush will help to give a soft shade and not let it become too harsh and bold. Shade around the ears, muzzle, mouth, tummy/chest crease, and bottom of foot. On tummy and foot areas, I also slightly stippled a faint bit of grey coloring to give a furry look. Load a liner brush into extender, then load with White Wash and pull wispy, small strokes in different directions on the chest to look like white hair or fur overlapping the black and shaded creases. Do the same thing on the head section where the head overlaps the ear and on the muzzle area along the shaded edges. Paint

wispy lines of Black around the eyes and along the bottom chin line. Load a liner brush into extender and load into Black, then stroke outward to form fine hairs around the eye and muzzle edge.

2. EYES AND NOSE: Basecoat with Black and highlight with sideload floats and dots of White Wash.

3. MUZZLE AND CHEEKS: Place tiny small whisker marks in the lower part of the muzzle using Black with extender in the brush. Moisten the muzzle with a satin film of extender, then touch into the Napthol Red Light and apply to the cheek areas, and immediately buff softly with a very soft touch.

4. PEPPERMINT: Roll a piece of Paperclay into a ball. Lay on a table and use a piece of wood to lay over the top and apply light pressure to flatten into the desired thickness and diameter. Allow to dry and sand smooth. (Refer to the Terms And Techniques section on the use of Creative Paperclay and Model Magic for more information.) Basecoat with White Wash and stripe with Napthol Red Light. Apply Heavenly Hues Glitter, then wrap with a small piece of iridescent cellophane tissue.

5. OBI AND SASH: I used a needle and thread to close up a piece of ribbon that is lapped over to size. I put a little piece of cotton ball inside for stuffing and closed the remaining area. Glue the obi onto the back and the sash across the tummy of the bear.

6. Shred the red and green curling ribbon into very thin strips and curl. Using metallic string, tie a small bow and grab up the holiday colors of ribbons. Glue to the head beside the left ear.

FINISHING
Glue all pieces together. Dry. Varnish.

POLAR BEAR COUSIN
COLOR PHOTO ON PAGE 4

PALETTE
DELTA CERAMCOAT
Black
Lt. Ivory
Pumpkin
DECOART AMERICANA
White Wash
LIQUITEX TUBE ACRYLIC ARTIST COLORS
Burnt Umber
JO SONJA'S ARTISTS' COLORS
Napthol Red Light

OTHER SUPPLIES
1/16" wide green satin ribbon
3 red jingle bells, 6mm
Creative Paperclay
FolkArt Extender
Metallic gold tie cording
Miniature icicle garland
Tacky Glue
Tiny gold eye screw
White fur doll hair

PREPARATION
Sand, seal, and sand again. Apply pattern for all basic design areas to be basecoated. (Re-apply pattern after basecoating is complete to define all features, body sections, creases, and folds, etc.) If you decide to place an icicle in the bear's hand as I have done, you will need to cut away one of the larger ones from the garland strand and place it across the hand area, letting it extend a small amount above the level of the hand and more extended below. Using the Creative Paperclay, mold an extension of the finger portions of the bear's hand around the icicle to appear that it is holding onto it. I also placed some Paperclay on the left ear for more dimension. (Refer to the Terms And Techniques section for more information on the use of Creative Paperclay and Model Magic.)

PAINTING PROCEDURE
1. BEAR FUR: Refer to the General Bear Instructions to familiarize yourself with the basic technique. This Polar bear will have fewer colors to work with to achieve the same stippled fur effect and highlights.

2. BEAR BODY: Basecoat entirely with Lt. Ivory, then re-apply the pattern as in all the rest of the Cubbies. Shade around all features, etc., using a mixture of a tiny tip of Black and even less Burnt Umber together. Begin stippling, using Lt. Ivory + White Wash over the entire bear. Add more White Wash for the next layer of stippling especially in the highlight areas. Re-shade where needed as we do in the final steps of painting the Cubbies. The eyes and nose will be the same; basecoated with Black and highlighted with White Wash. The cheeks will be the same also, brushing the extender over the muzzle to create a soft satin film of moisture. Tip this brush into Napthol Red Light and touch on upper cheeks, then immediately use a mop brush or dry, flat brush to buff the color to soften.

3. HAT: Basecoat with Napthol Red Light and doubleload highlight with Napthol Red Light and Pumpkin + a touch of Lt. Ivory. Shade with a mix of Napthol Red Light + a touch of Black to deepen the shade. (This could be Midnight Blue for the shading mix instead of Black.)

FINISH
Glue the miniature icicle garland around the waist area to look like a skirt. Glue and attach some of the White Furry Doll Hair/Trim along the hat band and a ball on the end of the hat. Thread the 1/16" wide green satin ribbon through three of the 6mm red jingle bells to form a necklace and attach at the neck. Next you will need to attach the arm cutout, which just does overlap the icicles, causing it not to fit flush with the wood body section. I stuffed a little Paperclay between the cutout and the body piece to help take up a bit of the void among the icicle tops. I feel that if you use the hot glue gun, it will give the thickness and filler to let the arm rest more easily into place. Dry. Varnish.

SWEET TREATS
COLOR PHOTO ON PAGE 31

PALETTE
DELTA CERAMCOAT
Black
Black Green
Bright Yellow
Empire Gold
Ivory
Maple Sugar Tan
Old Parchment
Spice Tan
Sunbright Yellow
Yellow
DECOART AMERICANA
Mistletoe
Ultra Blue Deep
White Wash
DECOART HEAVENLY HUES
Glitter
ACCENT COUNTRY COLORS
Raw Sienna
JO SONJA'S ARTISTS' COLORS
Napthol Red Light
LIQUITEX TUBE ACRYLIC ARTIST COLORS
Burnt Umber
OTHER SUPPLIES
1/16" wide yellow ribbon for bow
1/2" wide royal blue satin ribbon for bow
FolkArt Extender
Metallic gold tie cording
Palette knife
Snow-Tex Textural Medium
Tacky Glue
Tiny gold eye screw

PREPARATION
Sand, seal and sand again. Apply pattern for all basic design areas to be basecoated. (Re-apply pattern after the basecoating is completed to define all features, body sections, creases, folds, etc.)

PAINTING PROCEDURE
1. BEAR FUR: Basecoat with Spice Tan. Refer to the General Bear Instructions for the bear fur technique and specific palette that is used to complete the bear character.

2. ENTIRE CLOTHING: Basecoat with Ultra Blue Deep and doubleload highlights using Ultra Blue Deep and White Wash. The stars and stripes are Empire Gold. Shade with a sideload float of Black + Ultra Blue Deep.

3. FOOT PAD: Basecoat with White Wash and shade with Black. The dots are White Wash.

4. RED AND GREEN GUMDROPS AND LEMON WEDGE CANDY: Using a palette knife, apply a generous amount of Snow-Tex

to each candy. (Refer to the Terms And Techniques section under Snow-Tex for more details.) Dry. Paint using a sideload float of Mistletoe over the green gumdrops. Let the color be transparent to allow the highlight areas to show. Deepen the color in areas where needed using a stronger sideload of Mistletoe, then deepen further with a touch of Black Green. The red gumdrop is shaded with a sideload float of Napthol Red Light and then with a mix of Napthol Red Light + a touch of Ultra Blue Deepen to deepen the shaded areas. After all is dry, stipple a touch of White Wash for added highlights and a sugar coated texture. The lemon wedge has several shades of yellow. The inside skin is be the lightest, Sunbright Yellow. Then the triangle meat areas are Bright Yellow, shaded with Yellow. The outer skin is Yellow. Stipple a slight touch of White Wash on the lemon wedge. Apply Heavenly Hues Glitter for the final sparkle of sugar.

FINISH
Glue together all pieces. Dry. Varnish.

© debbie mitchell '96

RIBBON RIPPLE
COLOR PHOTO ON PAGE 31

PALETTE
DELTA CERAMCOAT
Black
Black Green
Hunter Green
Ivory
Maple Sugar Tan
Old Parchment
Pumpkin
Spice Tan
DECOART AMERICANA
Mistletoe
White Wash
DECOART HEAVENLY HUES
Glitter
ACCENT COUNTRY COLORS
Raw Sienna
JO SONJA'S ARTISTS' COLORS
Napthol Red Light
LIQUITEX TUBE ACRYLIC ARTIST COLORS
Burnt Umber

OTHER SUPPLIES
FolkArt Extender
Metallic gold tie cording
Tacky Glue
Tiny gold eye screw

PREPARATION
Sand, seal and sand again. Apply pattern for all basic design areas to be basecoated. (Re-apply pattern after the basecoating is completed to define all features, body sections, creases, folds, etc.)

PAINTING PROCEDURE
1. BEAR FUR: Basecoat with Spice Tan. Refer to the General Bear Instructions for the bear fur technique and specific palette that is used to complete the bear character.

2. RIBBON CANDY AND SHIRT: Basecoat with White Wash. Re-apply the pattern for the candy and major large stripes. The shirt has a small band that is trimmed along each sleeve and the collar with a liner brush using Hunter Green. The dots are done with a stylus dipped into Napthol Red Light. The shading is Black Green. The ribbon candy has larger stripes basecoated with Napthol Red Light and doubleload highlighted with Napthol Red Light and Pumpkin + a touch of Ivory. The double green lines on either side of the wider red stripe are painted with a liner brush using Mistletoe. Shade with a sideload float of Black Green. Dry. Apply Heavenly Hues Glitter.

3. UPPER BODICE SECTION OF OVERALLS: Basecoat with Napthol Red Light and doubleload highlight with Napthol Red Light and Pumpkin + a touch of Ivory. The stitches and buttons are Hunter Green.

4. LOWER PANTS SECTION: Basecoat with Hunter Green and doubleload highlights using Hunter Green and Mistletoe. Apply the plaid design with a #1 or #2 flat brush using White Wash. (Refer to the Terms And Techniques section that gives details for painting plaids and checks.) Use Napthol Red Light and a liner brush to line in the center of each White Wash stripe. All shading is painted with a sideload float of Black Green.

FINISH
Glue all pieces together. Dry. Varnish.

©debbie mitchell '96

LAP OF LUXURIES
COLOR PHOTO ON PAGE 31

PALETTE
DELTA CERAMCOAT
Black
Ivory
Maple Sugar Tan
Old Parchment
Spice Tan
DELTA RENAISSANCE FOIL
Adhesive
Green
Red
Silver
DECOART AMERICANA
White Wash
DECOART TRUE COLORS
Blue Violet
ACCENT COUNTRY COLORS
Raw Sienna
JO SONJA'S ARTISTS' COLORS
Napthol Red Light
LIQUITEX TUBE ACRYLIC ARTIST COLORS
Burnt Umber

OTHER SUPPLIES
1/16" wide red satin ribbon
5 tiny white buttons, 1/4" diameter or smaller
FolkArt Extender
Metallic gold tie cording
Red and white gingham check ribbon bow
Tacky Glue
Tiny gold eye screw

WOOD SOURCE
Miniature wooden doodads, such as the half acorn tops used for candy kisses may be purchased through:
Bear With Us, Inc.
8910 N. Greenhills Rd.
Kansas Cith, MO 64154-1501

PREPARATION
Sand, seal and sand again. Apply pattern for all basic design areas to be basecoated. (Re-apply pattern after the basecoating is completed to define all features, body sections, creases, folds, etc.)

PAINTING PROCEDURE
1. BEAR FUR: Basecoat with Spice Tan. Refer to the General Bear Instructions for the bear fur technique and specific palette that is used to complete the bear character.

2. COLLAR AND BOTTOM OF FOOT PAD: Basecoat with White Wash. Apply the tiny gingham check design on the collar with Napthol Red Light using a flattened liner brush. (Refer to the Terms And Techniques section for instructions on Painting Plaids And Checks.) Shading is done with a sideload float using a mix of Napthol Red Light + a touch of Blue Violet. The foot pad is shaded with Black, then dotted with White Wash.

3. PAJAMAS: Basecoat with Blue Violet. Doubleload highlights using Blue Violet and White Wash. Using either a liner brush or a #1 flat brush, apply the plaid design with Black. Shade with a sideload float of Black. The narrow red bands around the ankles and sleeve cuffs are Napthol Red Light.

4. KISSES CANDIES: Using Delta's Renaissance Foils and Adhesive, cover each of the wooden kisses. There is no need to basecoat these pieces for the look we are to achieve. First apply the adhesive. When it is no longer milky in color, apply a second coat. Allow to dry. With the shiny side up, apply the foil to the surface by pressing and rubbing with a finger or a pencil eraser. When you peel the paper away, it will leave the surface covered with the metallic finish. Lift and re-apply until completely covered.

5. STOOL: Stain with a wash of Burnt Umber, then sideload float the edges with a stronger color float of Burnt Umber.

FINISH
Using the 1/16" wide red satin ribbon, thread through the holes in the buttons to resemble thread. Glue the buttons into place on the ankle cuffs, on the arms, and in the center of the bow on the head. Tie a small red bow and attach to the center of the collar under the chin. Glue kisses into place. Dry. Varnish over entire bear and dimensional pieces.

TIGHT, STICKY SQUEEZE
COLOR PHOTO ON FRONT COVER

PALETTE
DELTA CERAMCOAT
Black
Black Green
Ivory
Maple Sugar Tan
Midnight Blue
Old Parchment
Spice Tan
DECOART AMERICANA
Mistletoe
Ultra Blue Deep
White Wash
DECOART HEAVENLY HUES
Glitter
ACCENT COUNTRY COLORS
Raw Sienna
JO SONJA'S ARTISTS' COLORS
Napthol Red Light
LIQUITEX TUBE ACRYLIC ARTIST COLORS
Burnt Umber

OTHER SUPPLIES
1/16" wide royal blue satin ribbon bow
1/8" wide green satin ribbon bow
FolkArt Extender
Metallic gold tie cording
Tacky Glue
Tiny gold eye screw

PREPARATION
Sand, seal and sand again. Apply pattern for all basic design areas to be basecoated. (Re-apply pattern after the basecoating is completed to define all features, body sections, creases, folds, etc.)

PAINTING PROCEDURE
1. BEAR FUR: Basecoat with Spice Tan. Refer to the General Bear Instructions for the bear fur technique and specific palette that is used to complete the bear character.

2. ENTIRE PAJAMA AREA: Basecoat with Mistletoe and doubleload highlight using Mistletoe and White Wash. The plaid design is painted with either a flattened liner brush or a #1 flat brush. The plaid is Ultra Blue Deep with thin Napthol Red Light lines between. The stitches on the toe areas and on the button panel are Ultra Blue Deep. The shading is done with a sideload float of Black Green. Using the small wood handle of a brush, dot buttons on the panel with Napthol Red Light.

3. CANDY CANE: Basecoat with White Wash. Apply the pattern for the stripes and basecoat with Napthol Red Light. When the width of the stripes are larger, as these are, you may wish to highlight using the color combination of Napthol Red Light doubleloaded with Pumpkin + a touch of Ivory. You can

use just the Napthol Red Light and White Wash alone as a reverse doubleload for each highlight on the red stripes. Shade using a sideload float of Midnight Blue + a touch of Black. Shade where the body overlaps the candy. The shadow line appears in the upper portion of the candy cane only. Apply a satin film of moisture on the candy surface using the extender. Tip the brush into Midnight Blue and place the shadow along one side, off-center. Immediately buff, lightly touching the surface, to soften the color using a mop brush or a dry, flat brush. Dry. Apply Heavenly Hues Glitter.

FINISH
Glue all parts and bows into place. Dry. Varnish.

TRIMMIN' THE TREE...OR IS THE TREE TRIMMIN' ME?!

COLOR PHOTO ON FRONT COVER

PALETTE

DELTA CERAMCOAT
Black
Crocus
Flesh Tan
Hunter Green
Ivory
Maple Sugar Tan
Midnight Blue
Mocha Brown
Old Parchment
Pumpkin
Spice Tan
Bright Yellow
DELTA CERAMCOAT GLEAMS
Kim Gold
DECOART AMERICANA
Forest Green
Mistletoe
Ultra Blue Deep
White Wash
DECOART HEAVENLY HUES
Glitter
ACCENT COUNTRY COLORS
Raw Sienna
JO SONJA'S ARTISTS' COLORS
Napthol Red Light
LIQUITEX TUBE ACRYLIC ARTIST COLORS
Burnt Umber

OTHER SUPPLIES

2 buttons, tan colored 1/4" diameter or smaller
FolkArt Extender
Jute string
Metallic gold tie cording
Model Magic of Creative Paperclay
Tacky Glue
Tiny gold eye screw

WOOD SOURCE

Miniature wooden doodads, such as the light bulbs and star tree topper may be purchased through:
Bear With Us, Inc.
8910 N. Greenhills Rd.
Kansas Cith, MO 64154-1501

PREPARATION

Sand, seal and sand again. Apply pattern for all basic design areas to be basecoated. (Re-apply pattern after the basecoating is completed to define all features, body sections, creases, folds, etc.)

PAINTING PROCEDURE

1. BEAR FUR: Basecoat with Spice Tan. Refer to the General Bear Instructions for the bear fur technique and specific palette that is used to complete the bear character.

2. PAJAMAS: Basecoat with Napthol Red Light. Doubleload highlight using Napthol Red Light and Pumpkin + a touch of Ivory. The liner work is Flesh Tan. Shade with a sideload float of a mix of Napthol Red Light + a touch of Midnight Blue.

3. TWO PATCHES ON SLEEVE: The right patch is basecoated with White Wash. The gingham checks are Hunter Green and the stripes are Napthol Red Light. The left patch is basecoated with Hunter Green. The snowflake pattern is White Wash. The stitches are Black.

4. HAT BAND: Basecoat with Napthol Red Light and highlight with a doubleload of Napthol Red Light and Pumpkin + a touch of Ivory. Stripe with Flesh Tan and shade with a sideload float of a mix of Napthol Red Light + a touch of Midnight Blue.

5. REMAINING PATCHWORK HAT: Starting at the top of the head, the first strip is basecoated with White Wash and the ticking stripes are Napthol Red Light. The second strip is basecoated with Hunter Green with a White Wash snowflake design. The third strip is basecoated with Napthol Red Light and has White Wash stripes. The fourth strip is basecoated with White Wash and has Hunter Green gingham checks. The fifth strip is basecoated with Flesh Tan and has a heart print of Napthol Red Light. The sixth strip is basecoated with Hunter Green and the plaid design is White Wash. The seventh strip is basecoated with Napthol Red Light and has Hunter Green plaid with Flesh Tan lines between. The eighth strip is basecoated with White Wash and has Napthol Red Light dots. The ninth and last strip is Basecoated with Hunter Green and has Flesh Tan dots. All shading is done with Black Green and the stitches are Black.

6. TREE: Basecoat with Forest Green and highlight with a doubleload of Forest Green and Mistletoe. Shade with a sideload float of Black Green. The trunk is basecoated with Spice Tan and shaded with Burnt Umber.

7. STAR CUTOUT TOPPER: Basecoat with Empire Gold and highlight with a doubleload of Empire Gold and Crocus. Using extender on a flat brush, load with a small amount of Mocha Brown and work onto the palette well. Shade one side of each star point. Apply Heavenly Hues Glitter.

8. SMALL WOODEN LIGHTS: There are twelve lights (two of each color). Basecoat with Napthol Red Light, Mistletoe, Ultra Blue Deep, White Wash, Pumpkin, and Bright Yellow. Basecoat the base portion of each bulb with Kim Gold. Apply Heavenly Hues Glitter to each bulb. Some of the bulbs were doubleload highlighted with the base color and White Wash to give a little highlight in certain places.

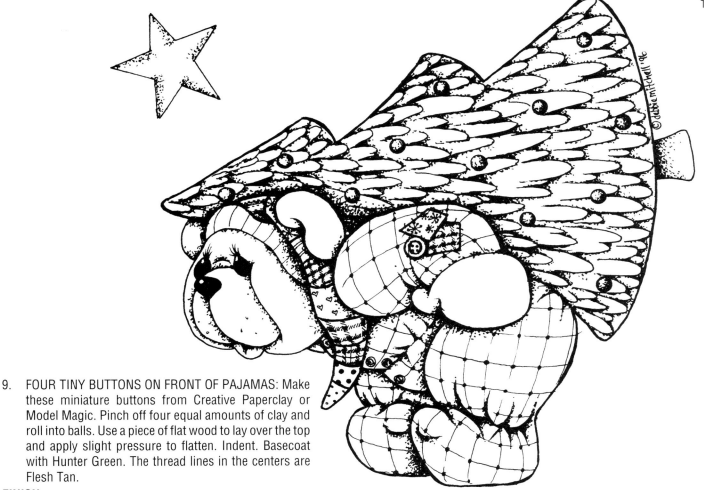

9. FOUR TINY BUTTONS ON FRONT OF PAJAMAS: Make these miniature buttons from Creative Paperclay or Model Magic. Pinch off four equal amounts of clay and roll into balls. Use a piece of flat wood to lay over the top and apply slight pressure to flatten. Indent. Basecoat with Hunter Green. The thread lines in the centers are Flesh Tan.

FINISH
Glue the star to the top of the tree. Secure the tiny bulbs with glue. Attach the one tan colored button at the end of the hat and the other one on the sleeve beside the patches. Take apart the threads of a piece of jute string and use one piece to make a couple of bows to attach to the ankles. Glue the four tiny buttons into place on the tummy. Dry. Varnish.

PUMPIN' PEPPERMINTS
COLOR PHOTO ON FRONT COVER

PALETTE
DELTA CERAMCOAT
Black
Ivory
Maple Sugar Tan
Old Parchment
Pumpkin
Spice Tan
DELTA CERAMCOAT GLEAMS
Kim Gold
DECOART AMERICANA
Leaf Green
Mistletoe
White Wash
DECOART TRUE COLORS
Blue Violet

DECOART HEAVENLY HUES
Glitter
ACCENT COUNTRY COLORS
Raw Sienna
JO SONJA'S ARTISTS' COLORS
Napthol Red Light
LIQUITEX TUBE ACRYLIC ARTIST COLORS
Burnt Umber

OTHER SUPPLIES
Creative Paperclay and/or Model Magic Modeling Compound
FolkArt Extender
Metallic gold tie cording
Piece of curling ribbon
Tacky Glue
Tiny gold eye screw

(CONTINUED ON PAGE 20)

PUMPIN' PEPPERMINTS
(CONTINUED FROM PAGE 19)

PREPARATION

Sand, seal and sand again. Apply pattern for all basic design areas to be basecoated. (Re-apply pattern after the basecoating is completed to define all features, body sections, creases, folds, etc.)

PAINTING PROCEDURE

1. BEAR FUR: Basecoat with Spice Tan. Refer to the General Bear Instructions for the bear fur technique and specific palette that is used to complete the bear character.

2. PANTS, LEFT HALF OF UPPER BODICE AND RIGHT SLEEVE: Basecoat with Napthol Red Light and highlight with a doubleload of Napthol Red Light and Pumpkin + a touch of Ivory. Apply the checks with a flattened liner brush using Black. (Refer to the Terms And Techniques section for instructions on painting plaids and checks.) Shade with a sideload float of Black.

3. RIGHT HALF OF UPPER BODICE AND LEFT HALF OF LOWER SHIRT: Basecoat with DecoArt Leaf Green and highlight with Mistletoe. Apply the Black checks as instructed in Step #2.

4. RIGHT HALF OF LOWER SHIRT, COLLAR, LEFT SLEEVE, AND UPPER LEG CUFF: Basecoat with Blue Violet and highlight with a heavy, well blended doubleload of Blue Violet and White Wash. Apply the Black checks as instructed in Step #2. Shade with Black. (Actually all shading could be done all at once when all checks are completed.)

5. SLEEVE CUFFS, NECK COLLAR BAND, AND LOWER ANKLE CUFFS: Basecoat with Black and highlight with White Wash.

6. DOWEL STICK: Basecoat with White Wash. (Refer to the Terms And Techniques section for instructions on Tips For Stripping Peppermint Candy Sticks.) These tips will explain how to stripe your dowel stick with Napthol Red Light. (Be sure to keep dowel through hand sections.)

7. PEPPERMINT CANDIES: The candies are formed from Creative Paperclay. Pinch off two equal portions of clay and roll into balls. Lay on table, place a piece of flat wood over top, and apply pressure until they both flatten to the desired diameter and thickness. Push onto the ends of the dowel stick. (NOTE: You may wish to do this step before painting the dowel stick. It is optional.) Dry completely. Basecoat with White Wash. The stripes are painted with a liner brush. Place sets of two stripes close together, then space, and repeat. When beginning each of these stripes, apply a very light touch for a thin line, add pressure for a slightly thicker line, then let up on pressure when ending the stroke. Before applying these stripes using Mistletoe, brush over the candies with extender. This will allow the stripes to slightly fuzz. Dry. Apply Heavenly Hues Glitter to each peppermint and the dowel stick.

8. FOUR BUTTONS: Using either Paperclay or Model Magic, pinch four tiny amounts of clay, roll into equal sized balls and flatten lightly. Indent slightly. Basecoat with Kim Gold and apply Black stitches in the center of each button.

FINISHING

Glue together all pieces. Dry. Varnish.

BUMPY RIDE
COLOR PHOTO ON PAGE 27

PALETTE
DELTA CERAMCOAT
Black
Black Green
Ivory
Maple Sugar Tan
Old Parchment
Spice Tan
DECOART AMERICANA
Mistletoe
White Wash
DECOART HEAVENLY HUES
Glitter
ACCENT COUNTRY COLORS
Raw Sienna
JO SONJA'S ARTISTS' COLORS
Napthol Red Light
LIQUITEX TUBE ACRYLIC ARTIST COLORS
Burnt Umber

OTHER SUPPLIES
2 gold jingle bells, 6mm
FolkArt Extender
Metallic gold tie cording (2 sizes; thin for bow with bells, medium for hanging ornament)
Tacky Glue
Tiny gold eye screw

PREPARATION
   Sand, seal and sand again. Apply pattern for all basic design areas to be basecoated. (Re-apply pattern after the basecoating is completed to define all features, body sections, creases, folds, etc.)

PAINTING PROCEDURE
1. BEAR FUR: Basecoat with Spice Tan. Refer to the General Bear Instructions for the bear fur technique and specific palette that is used to complete the bear character.

2. HAT, SHIRT SLEEVES, PANTS, AND SOCKS: Basecoat all areas with Mistletoe. Re-apply the basic pattern. Stripe the hat, sleeves and sock areas with White Wash. Highlight pants and bottom of foot pads using a doubleload of Mistletoe and White Wash. All shading is done with a sideload float of Black Green.

3. REMAINING SHIRT AREAS AND RIBBON CANDY: Basecoat shirt and candy with White Wash. Shade shirt with Black Green and dot button and collar band with Mistletoe. Apply the pattern for the ribbon candy and basecoat the large stripes with Mistletoe. Doubleload highlights with Mistletoe and White Wash. Using a liner brush, paint the small lines with Napthol Red Light and the double lines with Mistletoe. All shading is done with a sideload float using Black Green. Dry. Apply Heavenly Hues Glitter.

FINISH
   Using thin metallic cord to tie together 2 gold jingle bells and glue to the end of the hat. Towards the back edge of the toes, I applied small balls of the White Doll Hair/Trims to look like pompon balls. Dry. Varnish.

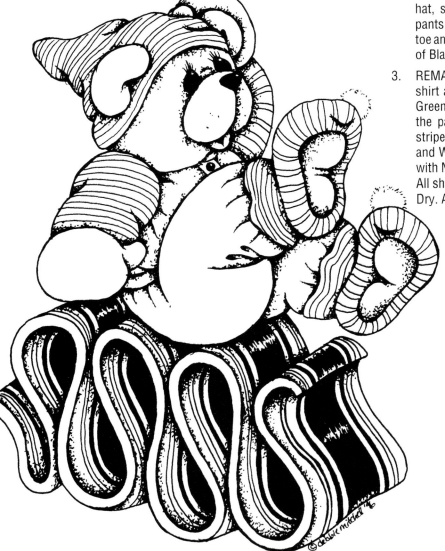

STICKIN' TO IT
COLOR PHOTO ON PAGE 60

PALETTE
DELTA CERAMCOAT
Black
Black Green
Hunter Green
Ivory
Maple Sugar Tan
Midnight Blue
Old Parchment
Spice Tan
DECOART AMERICANA
Leaf Green
White Wash
DECOART HEAVENLY HUES
Glitter
ACCENT COUNTRY COLORS
Raw Sienna
JO SONJA'S ARTISTS' COLORS
Napthol Red Light
LIQUITEX TUBE ACRYLIC ARTIST COLORS
Burnt Umber

OTHER SUPPLIES
1/8" wide hunter green satin ribbon
FolkArt Extender
Metallic gold tie cording
Model Magic
Tacky Glue
Tiny gold eye screw

PREPARATION
Sand, seal and sand again. Apply pattern for all basic design areas to be basecoated. (Re-apply pattern after the basecoating is completed to define all features, body sections, creases, folds, etc.)

PAINTING PROCEDURE
1. BEAR FUR: Basecoat with Spice Tan. Refer to the General Bear Instructions for the bear fur technique and specific palette that is used to complete the bear character.

2. SHIRT: Basecoat with Hunter Green and doubleload highlights using Hunter Green and White Wash. The snowflake design is painted with a liner brush using White Wash. Shade with a sideload float of Black Green.

3. OVERALLS: Basecoat with Napthol Red Light. Using a liner brush and White Wash, apply the plaid. Shade with a sideload float of Napthol Red Light + a touch of Midnight Blue.

4. FEET PADS: Basecoat with White Wash. Shade with a sideload float of Black + Midnight Blue. The dots are placed with a stylus using White Wash.

5. CANDY CANE: Basecoat with White Wash. Apply the pattern for the large stripes and then basecoat with Napthol Red Light. Doubleload highlights on each stripe using a reverse doubleload of Napthol Red Light and White Wash. (Refer to the pattern and color photo for highlight and shading placement.) Next, using a liner brush, place smaller green stripes on either side of the red stripes using DecoArt Americana Leaf Green. Shade along the body areas that overlap the candy using a mix of Black + Midnight Blue. The shadow line is achieved by first applying a satin film of extender to the candy surface. Then tip the corner of a flat brush into Midnight Blue and apply a strip of color along one side of the candy cane. Immediately use a mop brush or dry flat brush to lightly buff the color to soften. Dry. Apply Heavenly Hues Glitter.

6. TINY BUTTONS: Two buttons are made from Model Magic. Roll two small balls the same size. Flatten on top to the desired diameter with a piece of wood or something similar. Indent to form an outer rim. Basecoat with Hunter Green. The stitch in the center of each button is White Wash.

FINISH
Glue all pieces into place. Also glue on buttons and ribbon bow. Dry. Varnish.

SANTA CUBBY
COLOR PHOTO ON PAGE 60

PALETTE
DELTA CERAMCOAT
Black
Brown Iron Oxide
Ivory
Lt. Ivory
Maple Sugar Tan
Midnight Blue
Mocha Brown
Old Parchment
Pumpkin
Spice Tan
DELTA CERAMCOAT GLEAMS
Kim Gold
DECOART AMERICANA
Forest Green
Mistletoe
White Wash
ACCENT COUNTRY COLORS
Raw Sienna
JO SONJA'S ARTISTS' COLORS
Napthol Red Light
LIQUITEX TUBE ACRYLIC ARTIST COLORS
Burnt Umber

OTHER SUPPLIES
1/16" wide red satin ribbon
8 gold jingle bells, 6mm
All Cooped Up Stringlets, 1 pkg.
Creative Paperclay
FolkArt Extender
Metallic gold tie cording
Tacky Glue
Tiny gold eye screw

PREPARATION

Sand, seal and sand again. Apply pattern for all basic design areas to be basecoated. (Re-apply pattern after the basecoating is completed to define all features, body sections, creases, folds, etc.)

PAINTING PROCEDURE

1. BEAR FUR: Basecoat with Spice Tan. Refer to the General Bear Instructions for the bear fur technique and specific palette that is used to complete the bear character.

2. HAT AND SANTA SUIT: Basecoat with Napthol Red Light and doubleload highlights with Napthol Red Light and Pumpkin + a touch of Ivory. Sideload float shading with a mix of Napthol Red Light and a touch of Midnight Blue.

3. HANDS AND CANDY CANE: I chose to add dimension by adding paperclay to the hands and candy cane. Moisten the wood lightly with water and pinch off a small amount of clay. Place it in the center of the hand firmly, starting to press and smear toward the outer edges to adhere the clay tightly to the wood. Work with forming the shape of the hand and thumb area. (Refer to the Terms And Techniques section for more information and instructions for using Creative Paperclay and Model Magic.) When working with the candy cane/hand, form the candy cane first to have it ready to place in the hand, then form the remaining hand section to overlap the candy cane. To form the candy cane, roll the clay into a small snake-like roll. Cut to the size that is needed and bend the end to form a curve. When smoothing and shaping, use a brush dampened with water. Clean any residue off the bear using a cotton swab that has been dampened with water. Dry. Now you are ready to paint.

4. HANDS, BOOTS, AND BELT: Basecoat with Black. Highlight with a doubleload of Black and White Wash. Sideload float stronger highlights when necessary, then shade to clean up as well as to strengthen creases and divisions. The soles on the boots are basecoated with Brown Iron Oxide and doubleload highlighted with Mocha Brown on the edges. Shade with a sideload float of Burnt Umber. The buckle is basecoated with Kim Gold.

(CONTINUED ON PAGE 24)

SANTA CUBBY
(CONTINUED FROM PAGE 23)

5. FUR BANDS ON HAT AND SUIT: Basecoat with either Old Parchment or Ivory. You will be stippling as we do on the fur. The combinations of colors will go up through the following: Old Parchment + Ivory, then Ivory alone, next Ivory + Lt. Ivory. We want to let this fur have some layers, but not get too light in color to become white. The shade with Raw Sienna. Deepen the shading where needed with Burnt Umber. I tried to keep a more natural coloring to go with the beard. If you choose a beard material that is white, then make your painted fur areas more white in color. (I would then start with a lighter grey base and stipple layers of White.)

6. CANDY CANE: Basecoat with White Wash and stripe with Napthol Red Light.

7. CHAIR: Basecoat the fabric covered sections with Forest Green. Doubleload highlights using Forest Green and Mistletoe, then shade with a sideload float of Black Green. The gold tack heads are dots of Kim Gold. The wooden legs and frame are washed with a stain of Burnt Umber, then shaded with a sideload float of Burnt Umber.

FINISH

Glue the jingle bells into place. Tie a red satin bow and glue to the upper part of the candy cane. Cut apart the amount of Stringlets for the length needed to form the beard. Glue into place across the lower chin. Cut a few strings to length for the mustache and tie one strand in the center to divide. Glue this under the nose. Dry. Varnish.

PHOTOS OF SANTA AND ME!
COLOR PHOTO ON PAGE 60

Here is a special photo album to keep all those cherished collections of photos taken each year of your children or grandchildren sitting on Santa's lap. (NOTE: I chose to use my regular acrylic paints along with Delta Ceramcoat Textile Medium, rather than changing to fabric paints all together. This will be your decision and preference. I do use the fabric style brushes to paint on canvas or other fabric surfaces.)

PALETTE
DELTA CERAMCOAT
Black
Black Green
Brown Iron Oxide
Ivory
Lt. Ivory
Maple Sugar Tan
Midnight Blue
Old Parchment
Spice Tan
DELTA CERAMCOAT GLEAMS
Kim Gold
DECOART AMERICANA
Forest Green
White Wash
DECOART HEAVENLY HUES
Glitter
ACCENT COUNTRY COLORS
Raw Sienna
LIQUITEX TUBE ACRYLIC ARTIST COLORS
Burnt Umber
JO SONJA'S ARTISTS' COLORS
Napthol Red Light

OTHER SUPPLIES
2 gold jingle bells, 9mm
6 gold jingle bells, 6mm
All Cooped Up Stringlets, one pkg. for beard

Canvas photo album, 9" x 9"
Craft buttons, 2 red round 1/2", 2 green hearts 1/2",
    2 gold stars 1/2"
Delta Ceramcoat Textile Medium
Metallic gold tie cording, thin

SURFACE SOURCE
The 9" x 9" canvas photo album can be purchased from:

The Dalee Book Co.
267 Douglas St.
Brooklyn, NY 11217

PREPARATION
There is no preparation needed for the actual canvas surface other than applying the pattern. Normally on fabric, I re-trace the back side of the tracing of the pattern with a black pastel chalk pencil, then turn it over and place in position onto the shirt or whatever surface is being painted. Then, rubbing gently, releases the chalk onto the fabric, thus leaving you a pattern to go by. There are several ways to apply patterns. You may wish to use what works best for yourself. For this particular piece, since it has a different texture and hard backing, you may wish to use a lead pencil, re-trace the pattern on the back side, turn it over and use a stylus to transfer. You could also use a worn piece of black graphite paper and slip it under the pattern, then transfer using a stylus. (Be careful not to get the lines too bold or smudge where you hold the pattern in place with your fingers or you will get your album dirty!) Now, we are ready to paint! The differences between this piece and painting the wooden ornaments varies. One thing will be that we will not need to double load colors for highlighting. We will be applying the textile medium to each section to be painted before applying the paint and you may need to let each layer of stippling dry before moving onto the next highlight combination. Also, it will be a little more unforgiving! Take your time and think ahead. But, it's fun!

(INSTRUCTIONS CONTINUED ON PAGE 26)

Photo's of Santa and me!

PAINTING PROCEDURE

1. BEAR FUR: Basecoat with Spice Tan. Refer to the General Bear Instructions for the bear fur technique and specific palette that is used to complete the bear character. This same procedure is used with the color combinations. The only difference to be aware of is to let each layer dry before moving on or your colors will smash and blend together and you will lose the stippled fur look.

2. HAT AND SUIT: Basecoat with Napthol Red Light. Work with each separate section at a time. Pour textile medium onto your palette and dip the brush into it at all times. You may rinse your brush in water to clean it, but you will always load into medium first before painting. Apply this medium onto a section to be painted, such as the hat. This will moisten the fabric allowing you to softly blend your colors easily. Also, it will keep a more transparent, see through coloring which will serve as the highlights. Applying a stronger coverage of color (more pigment) towards the shaded areas will give you variations in the color to start to form your dimension in the painting. For this step, use the textile medium and Napthol Red Light. Now we want to add shading to the creases and folds. Make a mix of Napthol Red Light + a touch of Midnight Blue. This will be a deep burgundy color to shade with. Continue these steps throughout all red sections of the suit and hat. The remainder of your bear, chair, and camera design will follow the same procedure, but using different colors that are listed below.

3. HANDS, BELT, AND BOOTS: Basecoat with Black along with textile medium. Leave a more transparent bit of color for highlight areas as described in Step #2. This is why you have to pay attention and plan ahead while painting on fabrics. If needed, when dry, you may add a touch of a floated White Wash to accent come highlights that may be weak. The soles of the boots are basecoated with Brown Iron Oxide, then shaded with Burnt Umber. The buckle is basecoated with Kim Gold.

4. FUR COVERED BANDS ON HAT AND SUIT: Basecoat with Old Parchment or Maple Sugar. Stipple as we do with the bear fur, working with Old Parchment + Ivory, Ivory alone, then Ivory + a touch of Lt. Ivory. Keep this coloring close to the color of the natural canvas album and the Stringlets beard material. Shade with Raw Sienna and then deepen the shading with Burnt Umber.

5. CANDY CANE IN HAND: Basecoat with White Wash and stripe with Napthol Red Light. Apply Heavenly Hues Glitter.

6. CHAIR: The upper cloth covered portion is basecoated with Forest Green. Remember to apply thinner less pigment for a more transparent look to form the highlight areas. Apply heavier amounts of paint to start shading and variations of coloring. Next, shade using Black Green. The gold tack heads are dots of Kim Gold. The lower leg and frame portion of the chair is painted with Burnt Umber in the same procedure as stated in the last few steps.

7. CAMERA: The majority of the camera is painted using Burnt Umber and a mix of Black + White Wash to achieve a grey color, then shaded with Black. (Refer to the color photo for coloring and shading indications.)

8. LETTERING: Black.

9. STITCHES: Surrounding the outer edge of the book are stitches painted with Napthol Red Light and textile medium. Shade each end of each stitch with Black.

10. BUTTONS: I threaded each button with the thread from the Stringlets because of the natural color.

FINISH

Glue buttons, beard, and bells into place. Cut apart the amount of Stringlets needed to have the length for the beard. Spread across the face and glue into position. Cut a few strands to length for a mustache and tie a single strand in the center to divide it. Glue this under the nose area.

YIPPEE! MERRY CHRISTMAS!
COLOR PHOTO ON PAGE 27

PALETTE
DELTA CERAMCOAT

Black	Midnight Blue
Black Green	Old Parchment
Ivory	Spice Tan
Maple Sugar Tan	

DECOART AMERICANA
Leaf Green
Mistletoe
White Wash
DECOART HEAVENLY HUES
Glitter
ACCENT COUNTRY COLORS
Raw Sienna
JO SONJA'S ARTISTS' COLORS
Napthol Red Light

LIQUITEX TUBE ACRYLIC ARTIST COLORS
Burnt Umber

OTHER SUPPLIES
FolkArt Extender
Metallic gold string
Metallic gold tie cording
Model Magic Modeling Compound
Tacky Glue
Tiny gold eye screw

PREPARATION
Sand, seal, and sand again. Apply pattern for all basic design areas to be basecoated. (Re-apply pattern after the basecoating is completed to define all features, body sections, creases, folds, etc.)

(CONTINUED ON PAGE 28)

HOLIDAY CHRISTMAS ANGEL JARBRIGHT LAMP Pages 42 and 43
YIPPEE! MERRY CHRISTMAS! Pages 26 and 28
HANGIN' ON TIGHT Page 29
BUMPY RIDE Page 21

PAINTING PROCEDURE

1. BEAR FUR: Basecoat with Spice Tan. Refer to the General Bear Instructions for the bear fur technique and specific palette that is used to complete the bear character.

2. SLEEVES, BODY SECTION, AND LEGS: Basecoat with DecoArt Americana's Leaf Green. Highlight using a doubleload of Leaf Green and Mistletoe. Apply plaid on body section using a liner brush and White Wash. (Refer to the color photo, the Terms And Techniques section, and the pattern.) Shade all green areas with Black Green.

3. COLLAR AND ANKLE BOW: Basecoat with Napthol Red Light. Highlight with a doubleload of Napthol Red Light and a mix of Pumpkin + Ivory. The plaid lines are applied with White Wash using a liner brush. Shade with a deep burgundy color mix of Napthol Red Light + a touch of Midnight Blue. The stitches around the outer edges of the collar are Black Green or you can use Black.

4. CANDY CANE: Basecoat with White Wash. Apply the pattern for the stripes and basecoat with alternating colors using Mistletoe and Napthol Red Light. (Refer to the pattern and color photo for stripe color placement, highlights, and shading areas.) Highlight with a doubleload of Mistletoe and White Wash for the green stripes and Napthol Red Light and White Wash for the red stripes. Each highlight is placed with a reverse doubleload stroke inside each individual stripe, keeping the highlight color inside toward the center. Shade with a sideload float using Black Green along the tummy edge where it overlaps the candy cane. The shadow line that helps give the illusion of the candy cane being rounded is done by brushing extender over the area until you have a satin film of moisture on the surface. Tip a corner of the brush into Midnight Blue and stroke along the shadow line indicated on the pattern. Immediately use a mop brush or dry, flat brush to buff out the color to soften. When dry, apply Heavenly Hues Glitter over the entire candy cane.

5. BUTTONS AND MERRY CHRISTMAS BEAD BLOCKS: I chose to use Model Magic Modeling Compound for these items instead of Creative Paperclay. (Although the Paperclay may very well be used if preferred.) The Paperclay will tend to crack along the edges of the buttons, especially when formed. This will mean more working and smoothing with moist fingers and brushes, being careful not to get the buttons out of shape. First, determine the size of the buttons and beads. Pull off tiny amounts, trying to keep them the same size. Roll into round balls first. For buttons, lay on a flat surface, (such as the table), use a piece of flat board or surface and lay it over the top of all the little balls that are to be buttons and apply light pressure to flatten them all at the same time to the same thickness and diameter. Next, using an object that is smaller in diameter, such as a smaller dowel stick, indent the buttons slightly, to form an outer rim on the buttons. They will then be ready to paint with the desired color and thread in an alternating, matching color. I left these particular buttons and beads the natural white color of the Model Magic. If using the Paperclay, basecoat with White Wash. Use both your index fingers and thumbs together to form the remaining round balls into squares, alternating on all six sides. Using a needle or the needle type tool from the sculpting tool set, poke holes through each bead then thread through with tiny, fine gold metallic string. Attach from hand to hand. The lettering is painted with Black using a liner brush. You may wish to try the Pigma Waterproof Pen, (be careful not to bare down too hard). There are 15 beads. One bead is a spacer between the words and it has holly leaves and berries painted on it. There are 3 buttons; 2 on the collar and 1 on the ankle bow. Paint the thread in the center of each button with Napthol Red Light.

FINISH
Glue together all pieces and buttons in place. Dry. Varnish.

HANGIN' ON TIGHT
COLOR PHOTO ON PAGE 27

PALETTE
DELTA CERAMCOAT
Black
Black Green
Hunter Green
Ivory
Lt. Ivory
Maple Sugar Tan
Midnight Blue
Old Parchment
Pumpkin
Spice Tan
DECOART AMERICANA
Mistletoe
White Wash
DECOART HEAVENLY HUES
Glitter
ACCENT COUNTRY COLORS
Raw Sienna
JO SONJA'S ARTISTS' COLORS
Napthol Red Light
LIQUITEX TUBE ACRYLIC ARTIST COLORS
Burnt Umber

OTHER SUPPLIES
1 green 1/2" diameter button
1 off white 3/8" button
FolkArt Extender
Metallic gold tie cording
Red and green threads for buttons
Tacky Glue
Tiny gold eye screw

PREPARATION
Sand, seal, and sand again. Apply pattern for all basic design areas to be basecoated. (Re-apply pattern after the basecoating is completed to define all features, body sections, creases, folds, etc.)

PAINTING PROCEDURE
1. BEAR FUR: Basecoat with Spice Tan. Refer to the General Bear Instructions for the bear fur technique and specific palette that is used to complete the bear character.

2. BODY/LEG SECTIONS: Basecoat with Napthol Red Light. Highlight with a doubleload using Napthol Red Light and a mix of Pumpkin + a touch of Ivory. Shading on this section of the body will be done with a sideload float using a mix of Napthol Red Light + a touch of Midnight Blue.

3. TIP ENDS OF TOE AREAS: Basecoat with Hunter Green. Doubleload highlights using Hunter Green and Mistletoe. Shade with Black Green. The stitches are Lt. Ivory.

4. ARM SLEEVE, FOOT PAD, AND HIP PATCH: Basecoat with Lt. Ivory. Alternate colors of Napthol Red Light and Hunter Green when applying the check/plaid design. Use a liner or

#1 flat brush, referring to the Terms And Techniques section for further instruction. Shade with a sideload float of Black Green. Shade the foot pad with a mix of Black + Midnight Blue, then apply the dots using a stylus and Lt. Ivory.

5. BUTTONS ON TUMMY, BUTTON HOLES, AND STITCHES: All these items are painted with Lt. Ivory.

6. CANDY CANE: Basecoat with White Wash. Apply the pattern for the larger stripes, then basecoat them with Mistletoe. Doubleload highlight the center of each each stripe using Mistletoe and White Wash, keeping the highlight side of the brush toward the center of the highlight area, reversing the brush back and forth. Refer to the pattern and color photo for this placement. With a liner brush and Napthol Red Light place three thin lines between each green stripe. Shade on the candy cane against where any of the body overlaps the candy using Black Green. The shadow line off one side of the candy cane is done using extender. Brush on extender back and forth over and over the entire candy surface until you achieve a satin film of moisture. Tip a corner of the brush into Midnight Blue and stroke along the shadow line indicated on the pattern. Using a mop brush or a dry flat brush, immediately buff out the color with a soft touch. When dry, apply the Heavenly Hues Glitter.

FINISH
Glue together all pieces and buttons beside patch. Dry. Varnish.

LAZY LICKIN'S
COLOR PHOTO ON PAGE 31

PALETTE

DELTA CERAMCOAT
Black
Black Green
Ivory
Maple Sugar Tan

Midnight Blue
Old Parchment
Spice Tan

DECOART AMERICANA
Leaf Green
Mistletoe
White Wash
DECOART HEAVENLY HUES
Glitter
ACCENT COUNTRY COLORS
Raw Sienna
JO SONJA'S ARTISTS' COLORS
Napthol Red Light
LIQUITEX TUBE ACRYLIC ARTIST COLORS
Burnt Umber

OTHER SUPPLIES

FolkArt Extender
Metallic gold tie cording
Small bow, red with white dots
Tacky Glue
Tiny gold eye screw

PREPARATION

Sand, seal and sand again. Apply pattern for all basic design areas to be basecoated. (Re-apply pattern after the basecoating is completed to define all features, body sections, creases, folds, etc.)

PAINTING PROCEDURE

1. BEAR FUR: Basecoat with Spice Tan. Refer to the General Bear Instructions for the bear fur technique and specific palette that is used to complete the bear character.

2. UPPER BODICE AND UPPER SLEEVE: Basecoat with White Wash and stripe with Napthol Red Light.

3. FEET PADS: Basecoat with White Wash, shade with Black, then dot with White Wash.

4. LOWER PAJAMA AREA: Basecoat with DecoArt Leaf Green and double load highlight with Leaf Green and Mistletoe. Shade with a sideload float of Black Green. The belt at the waistline is Napthol Red Light and so is the cuff on the bottom of the sleeve.

5. KNEE PATCH, BACK FLAP, AND LOWER SLEEVE: Basecoat with White Wash first. Divide each area off into the small square patches. Start filling in the color combinations. Some squares are basecoated with Napthol Red Light. Some are divided in half diagonally and some into quarters. In these red squares some have been striped and dotted with White Wash. The hearts are White Wash also. Some red squares have Leaf Green Trees. Leave some squares white. The white squares have several designs such as Napthol Red Light gingham checks, stripes, checkerboard checks, and dots. Some of the white squares have Leaf Green details, including plaid lines, gingham checks, and dots. Some squares are basecoated with Leaf Green with Napthol Red Light dots, White Wash checks, and White Wash stripes. Some are left solid green. There is a Leaf Green band dividing the lower patchwork portion of the sleeve from the upper stripped portion. Apply a touch of Mistletoe for highlight if needed. All shading is Black Green

6. CANDY CANE: Basecoat with White Wash, then apply the pattern for the stripes. All stripes are Napthol Red Light. Highlight the larger red stripes either with a doubleload of Napthol Red Light and White Wash or with Napthol Red Light and Pumpkin + a touch of

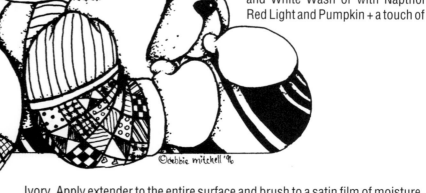

Ivory. Apply extender to the entire surface and brush to a satin film of moisture. Tip a flat brush into Midnight Blue and apply the shadow line. Using a mop brush or dry flat brush, buff the color to soften. Apply Heavenly Hues Glitter.

FINISH
Glue the pieces together. Dry. Varnish.

Mmm...ICIN' COOKIES
COLOR PHOTO ON PAGE 30

PALETTE
DELTA CERAMCOAT
Black
Black Green
Ivory
Maple Sugar Tan
Mocha Brown
Old Parchment
Pumpkin
Spice Tan
DECOART AMERICANA
Leaf Green
Mistletoe
White Wash
DECOART HEAVENLY HUES
Glitter
ACCENT COUNTRY COLORS
Raw Sienna
JO SONJA'S ARTISTS' COLORS
Napthol Red Light
LIQUITEX TUBE ACRYLIC ARTIST COLORS
Burnt Umber

OTHER SUPPLIES
FolkArt Extender
Metallic gold tie cording
S'getti String, green, 1" length
Stencil for tiny checks
Tacky Glue
Tiny gold eye screw

PREPARATION
Sand, seal and sand again. Apply pattern for all basic design areas to be basecoated. (Re-apply pattern after the basecoating is completed to define all features, body sections, creases, folds, etc.)

PAINTING PROCEDURE
1. BEAR FUR: Basecoat with Spice Tan. Refer to the General Bear Instructions for the bear fur technique and specific palette that is used to complete the bear character.

2. DECORATING TUBE AND FOOT PAD: Basecoat with White Wash. The shading is a sideload float of Black. Dot the foot pad with a stylus using White Wash. The tip of the tube is basecoated with a grey mix of Black + White Wash and shaded with Black. Highlight with White Wash.

3. PAJAMAS AND TONGUE: Basecoat with Napthol Red Light. Doubleload highlight with Napthol Red Light and Pumpkin + Ivory. The sleeves and open flap are stenciled with White Wash checks. The button holes are White Wash. All shading is done with a mix of Napthol Red Light + a touch of Black Green or Midnight Blue. The tongue is highlighted and shaded the same as the pajamas.

4. COOKIE: Basecoat with Old Parchment. Shade with Mocha Brown, then deepen the shading with Burnt Umber. The green icing is DecoArt Leaf Green, highlighted with Mistletoe and shaded with Black Green. Dot with Napthol Red Light, then apply tiny highlight dot of White Wash on each red dot.

5. CHAIR: Stain with a wash of Burnt Umber. The shading is done with a stronger sideload float of Burnt Umber to indicate the details. The inside openings are basecoated with Black Green.

FINISH
Glue S'getti string piece into the end of the decorating tube and cut off just long enough to let the string curve and lodge against the cookie freely. This will give the illusion that the icing is flowing from the tube onto the cookie. Varnish.

GIDDY-UP!
COLOR PHOTO ON PAGE 30

PALETTE
DELTA CERAMCOAT
Black
Crocus
Ivory
Maple Sugar Tan
Midnight Blue
Old Parchment
Pumpkin
Spice Tan
DECOART AMERICANA
White Wash

DECOART HEAVENLY HUES
Glitter
ACCENT COUNTRY COLORS
Raw Sienna
JO SONJA'S ARTISTS' COLORS
Napthol Red Light
LIQUITEX TUBE ACRYLIC ARTIST COLORS
Burnt Umber

OTHER SUPPLIES
1 red jingle bell, 6mm
Creative Paperclay
FolkArt Extender
Metallic gold tie cording
Tacky Glue
Thread and needle
Tiny gold eye screw

PREPARATION

Sand, seal and sand again. Apply pattern for all basic design areas to be basecoated. (Re-apply pattern after the basecoating is completed to define all features, body sections, creases, folds, etc.)

PAINTING PROCEDURE

1. BEAR FUR: Basecoat with Spice Tan. Refer to the General Bear Instructions for the bear fur technique and specific palette that is used to complete the bear character.

ENTIRE NIGHTGOWN AND NIGHTCAP: Basecoat with Napthol Red Light. Highlight the hat band, cuffs, and button flap with a doubleload of Napthol Red Light and a mix of Pumpkin + a touch of Ivory. Using a liner brush, apply small Black stitches to the border of each of these areas. Either use a #1 flat brush or a #1 liner brush, which has been flattened when loading, to form the Black checks on the remaining hat and gown. (Refer to the Terms And Techniques section for further instructions on Painting Plaids And Checks.) Once this process has been completed, shade with a sideload float using Black.

3. CANDY CANE: Basecoat with White Wash. Apply the pattern for the stripes and basecoat the large stripes with Napthol Red Light. Follow the pattern and color photo for correct placement for highlights and shading. Highlight each red stripe using with a doubleload of Napthol Red Light and a mix of Pumpkin + Ivory, reversing the brush back and forth with

(CONTINUED ON PAGE 36)

GIDDY-UP!
(CONTINUED FROM PAGE 35)

the highlight side of the brush always to the center. The shading under the feet is done with a sideload float mix of Midnight Blue + a slight touch of Black, using the corner of a flat brush. To apply the shadow side of the candy cane, brush on a satin film of extender, touch the corner of a flat brush into Midnight Blue and stroke along the shadow line. Immediately use a mop brush or a dry, soft, flat brush and buff to soften the color. Dry completely, then apply Heavenly Hues Glitter.

4. MAKING POPCORN STRAND: Form irregular shapes from the Paperclay to resemble popcorn. Lay them out on waxed paper or palette paper to dry. When totally dry, use a needle and heavy duty thread to string the pieces together to form a strand. Basecoat the entire strand with White Wash. Using Spice Tan and a liner brush, form what looks like the inside kernels of the popcorn. Lightly wash over parts of the popcorn pieces with Crocus to give a slight buttered look.

FINISH
Glue everything into place. Varnish.

STRINGIN' THINGS
COLOR PHOTO ON PAGE 30

PALETTE
DELTA CERAMCOAT
Black
Hunter Green
Ivory
Maple Sugar Tan
Midnight Blue
Old Parchment
Spice Tan
DECOART AMERICANA
Santa Red
White Wash
ACCENT COUNTRY COLORS
Raw Sienna
JO SONJA'S ARTISTS' COLORS
Napthol Red Light
LIQUITEX TUBE ACRYLIC ARTIST COLORS
Burnt Umber

OTHER SUPPLIES
1/16" wide green satin ribbon for bows
3 gold jingle bells, 6mm
Creative Paperclay
FolkArt Extender
Metallic gold tie cording
Tacky Glue
Thread and needle
Tiny gold eye screw

PREPARATION
Sand, seal and sand again. Apply pattern for all basic design areas to be basecoated. (Re-apply pattern after the basecoating is completed to define all features, body sections, creases, folds, etc.)

PAINTING PROCEDURE

1. BEAR FUR: Basecoat with Spice Tan. Refer to the General Bear Instructions for the bear fur technique and specific palette that is used to complete the bear character.

2. OVERALLS, CUFFS, AND HAT: Basecoat with Santa Red and doubleload highlight with Santa Red and Pumpkin + a touch of Ivory. Shade with a sideload float of Santa Red + a touch of Midnight Blue. The stitches are Ivory.

3. SLEEVES, HAT BAND, SHIRT, AND BOOTS: Basecoat with Hunter Green and doubleload highlight with Hunter Green and White Wash. Shade with a sideload float of Black Green. The stitches are Ivory.

4. PAPERCLAY POPCORN AND CRANBERRIES: Using Creative Paperclay, form the popcorn shapes. (Refer to the Terms And Techniques section for instructions on the use of Creative Paperclay and Model Magic.) To form the cranberries, pinch off 8 equal sized balls of Paperclay and roll into balls, then work into a more oval shape. Make a hole through each piece while still wet. Let all dry, then use a needle and thread to string all together. Basecoat the popcorn with White Wash. Paint inside the opening with Spice Tan to look like the kernel area. Shade in some kernels with Burnt Umber, if needed. Lightly and faintly wash the popcorn with Crocus for a buttered look. The cranberries are basecoated with Santa Red.

FINISH
Glue together all cutout pieces. Tie a tiny green bow and glue a jingle bell in the center for each toe and at the end of the hat. A single bow and ribbon strip is glued at the waist. Glue one end of the string of popcorn and cranberries to each hand so that it hangs in front of the bear. Dry. Varnish.

©debbie mitchell

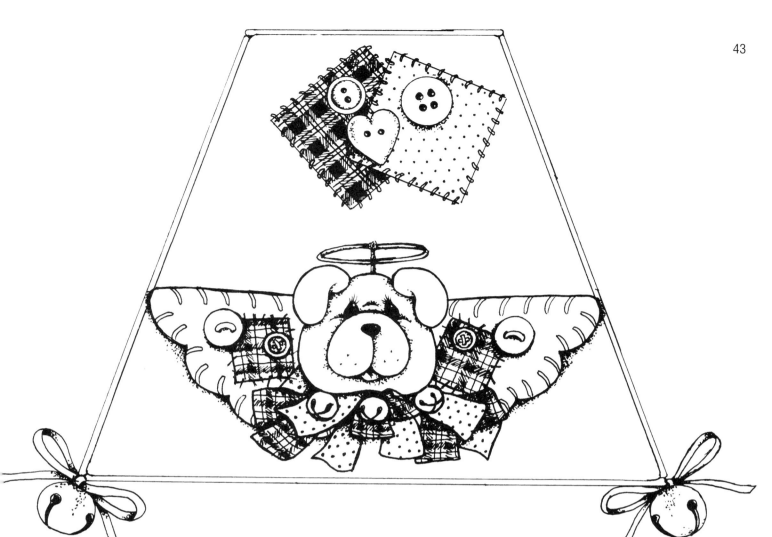

CELESTIAL CUBBY COLLECTIBLES

A few more angels are added for your home decor to be used as plant sticks to place throughout your poinsettias or other house plants adding to the overall Christmas spirit! Of course, you may prefer to create an arrangement similar to the photo for your decorating needs. If you desire, you may reduce these designs slightly and have additional ornaments to continue the collection. These particular designs do not limit decorating for "just Christmas." A few slight changes, such as miniature sunflowers instead of poinsettias, and you're set for year 'round enjoyment!

GINGERBREAD GOODIES
COLOR PHOTO ON PAGE 57

PALETTE
DELTA CERAMCOAT
Black
Black Green
Burnt Sienna
Flesh Tan
Ivory
DECOART AMERICANA
Forest Green
White Wash

Maple Sugar Tan
Mocha Brown
Old Parchment
Spice Tan

DECOART DIMENSIONS
Christmas Green
White Iridescent
ACCENT COUNTRY COLORS
Raw Sienna
JO SONJA'S ARTISTS' COLORS
Napthol Red Light
LIQUITEX TUBE ACRYLIC ARTIST COLORS
Burnt Umber

(CONTINUED ON PAGE 44)

GINGERBREAD GOODIES
(CONTINUED FROM PAGE 43)

OTHER SUPPLIES

Black wire, double braided twisted, for halo
Craft buttons, 2 green 1/2", 2 black 1/4", 4 ivory 1/4"
Creative Paperclay
DecoArt Snow-Tex Textural Medium
Fabric strips, green/black gingham check
FolkArt Extender
Hot glue gun
Old toothbrush
Pigma Micron waterproof fine line pen
Tacky Glue

WOOD SOURCE

Miniature wooden doodads, such as book and cookie shapes may be purchased through:

Bear With Us, Inc.
8910 N. Greenhills Rd.
Kansas City, MO 64154-1501

PREPARATION

Sand, seal and sand again. Apply pattern for all basic design areas to be basecoated. (Re-apply pattern after the basecoating is completed to define all features, body sections, creases, folds, etc.)

PAINTING PROCEDURE

1. BEAR FUR: Basecoat with Spice Tan. Refer to the General Bear Instructions for the bear fur technique and specific palette that is used to complete the bear character.

2. ENTIRE DRESS, RUFFLES, APRON, WINGS, AND BLOOMERS: Basecoat with Flesh Tan. Highlight all sections, creases and folds using a doubleload of Flesh Tan and Ivory. Shading on the collar, cuffs, apron, dress ruffle, and bloomers is sideload floated by using extender on a flat brush and loading into Mocha Brown. Blend well and softly on palette before placing on design. Dry. Deepen the shading in some areas using Burnt Umber. The wings and apron have a light spattering misted on the surface using an old toothbrush and thinned Burnt Umber (Refer to the Terms And Techniques section for more complete instructions for Spattering.) There are tiny Black stitches along the bottom edge of the apron.

3. DRESS DETAILS: Apply the tiny gingham check design using a flattened liner brush. (Refer to the Terms And Techniques section for more information concerning Painting Plaids And Checks.) This color will be Forest Green. All shading on these gingham areas is done with Black Green.

4. DETAILS ON WINGS: Using Christmas Green dimensional paint, place the stitches around the outer edges of the wings. Start each stroke about 3/8" from the edge on the front side.

Continue to pull and squeeze the bottle gently and evenly over the top cut edge of the wing before stopping. I arranged a cluster of three craft buttons on each side of the wings, using green, black, and ivory round shaped buttons.

5. HANDS, MINIATURE WOODEN BOOK, AND GINGERBREAD COOKIES: The hands are formed using Creative Paperclay. These will need to be made and attached after the cookies and book are completed and ready to place onto the front of the bear. The cookies are miniature wood cutouts covered with a thin amount of Snow-Tex. I use a palette knife to apply the Snow-Tex completely around each one. Dry. Paint with a basecoat coverage using a mix of Burnt Sienna + a touch of Mocha Brown. Dry again. Then decorate simply with the application of the White Iridescent dimensional paint. The cook book is basecoated with White Wash first. Use a #1 or #2 flat brush and Napthol Red Light to apply the diagonal checks over the cover of the entire book. The inside page areas are left white as well as the title square at the top of the front cover. The lettering is painted with Black using a liner brush. A fine line permanent pen may be used also. I worked with arranging my miniature objects into place, then I glued them to anchor before placing the hands permanently.

6. FORMING HANDS: (Refer to the Terms And Techniques section for detailed instructions on working with Creative Paperclay and Model Magic.) Using the Paperclay, pinch off two equal amounts of the clay. Form into shape by referring to the color photo and the pattern. Attach by moistening the bear cutout surface with water and pressing firmly into position, but not too hard as to disfigure! It may be beneficial to add a touch of your Tacky Glue to secure the hands better. Pinch and smear the edge of the clay onto the wood so that it will secure, but also they will appear to be part of the wood and character and not just a piece glued on. Clean up by using a wet brush, working at the outer residue and pushing it all back towards the hands. Not only will this clean up, but it will also help secure the edges. The residue can be cleaned as you work and while it is still moist or after it has dried it will reactivate with water on a cotton swab. Curl the hands so they rest over the cookies and look as if they are comfortably nestled in her "lovin' arms!" Dry. Paint the hands with a basecoat of Spice Tan and follow the instructions for the fur. I formed a tiny button from the Paperclay also. Roll a small piece of Paperclay into a ball, press to flatten slightly, indent, and basecoat with Flesh Tan.

FINISH

Assemble remaining pieces. Glue wings into place and secure the halo with a touch of glue also. The halo is a piece of black colored double-braid wire formed around a paint bottle lid for proper diameter. Glue the tiny button at the upper dress area and cut strips about 1/2" wide of the green and black gingham fabric. Tie the fabric strips into small bows. Hot glue onto the gathered ankle areas of the bloomers then glue a small ivory colored button in the center of each bow in top of the knot. Varnish.

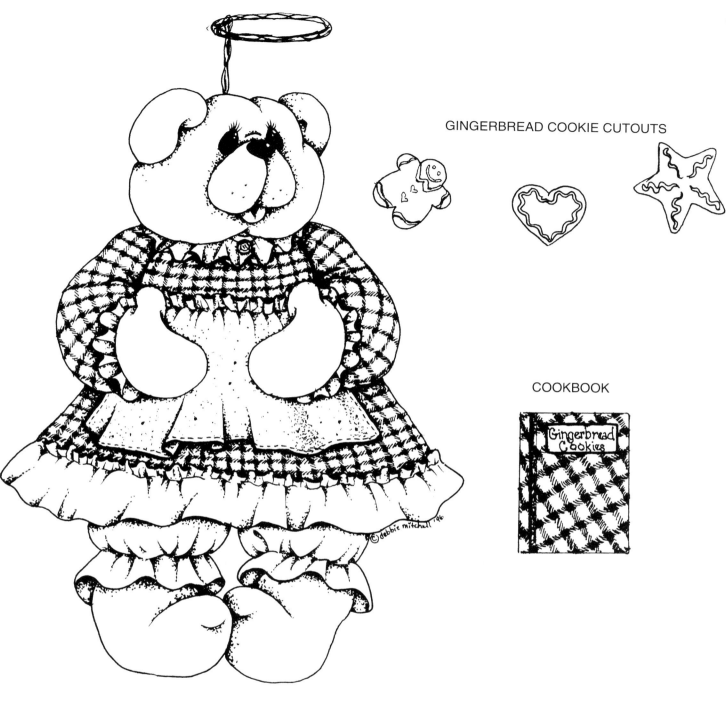

GINGERBREAD COOKIE CUTOUTS

COOKBOOK

Gingerbread Cookies

ANGEL WINGS

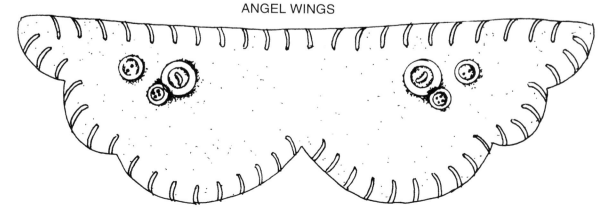

FOOTLOOSE 'N HEAVENLY!
COLOR PHOTO ON PAGE 57

PALETTE
DELTA CERAMCOAT
Black
Crocus
Empire Gold
Ivory
Lt. Ivory

Maple Sugar Tan
Midnight Blue
Mocha Brown
Old Parchment
Spice Tan

DELTA CERAMCOAT GLEAMS
Pearl Finish
DECOART AMERICANA
Leaf Green
Mistletoe
White Wash
DECOART HEAVENLY HUES
Glitter
ACCENT COUNTRY COLORS
Raw Sienna
LIQUITEX TUBE ACRYLICS
Burnt Umber
JO SONJA'S ARTISTS' COLORS
Napthol Red Light

OTHER SUPPLIES
20 gauge gold craft wire for halo
Craft buttons, 1 each green and white or light ivory 1/2",
        1 green 1/4"
Creative Paperclay or Model Magic
FolkArt Extender
Hot glue gun
Miniature garland greenery
Natural sea sponge
Tacky Glue

WOOD SOURCE
Miniature wooden doodads, such as star cutouts may be purchased through:

Bear With Us, Inc.
8910 N. Greenhills Rd.
Kansas City, MO 64154-1501

PREPARATION
Sand, seal and sand again. Apply pattern for all basic design areas to be basecoated. (Re-apply pattern after the basecoating is completed to define all features, body sections, creases, folds, etc.)

PAINTING PROCEDURE
1. BEAR FUR: Basecoat with Spice Tan. Refer to the General Bear Instructions for the bear fur technique and specific palette that is used to complete the bear character.

2. WINGS, DRESS, SHIRT AND LEGS: Basecoat all with Lt. Ivory. Brush on the Pearl Finish over the shirt and legs. The wings have been sponged over the top of the Lt. Ivory base color, first using White Wash, then using Pearl Finish in places over this. Next, coat entirely with Heavenly Hues Glitter and place a ric-rac design bordering the outer edges using a liner brush and Midnight Blue. Attached in the center void opening of the left half of the wing will be the green and white clusters of buttons. The shirt has a Midnight Blue ric-rac design placed at the bottom edge of each sleeve. Apply a very tiny print using a liner brush and DecoArt Leaf Green in the 3-stroke clusters. There is a single dot of Napthol Red Light in each stroke cluster. Shade with a mix of Midnight Blue + a touch of Black.

3. LEG AND FEET AREAS: Shade the creases with a mix of Midnight Blue + a touch of Black on the Lt. Ivory areas as we did on the shirt. The toe and heel sections are basecoated with Leaf Green and highlighted with a doubleload of Leaf Green and Mistletoe. Shade with sideload floats of Black Green. Using a liner brush, apply black stitches. The bottoms of the feet are shaded with the blue/black mix also.

4. JUMPER: The entire jumper has the gingham checks or plaid look that varies in sizes. (Refer to the Terms And Techniques section for a more detailed explanation of Painting Plaids And Checks.) The very uppermost segment of the bodice, straps, and pocket are done with a flattened liner brush for a very small gingham checked look. The remaining jumper has a larger check painted with a #1 or #2 flat brush and spaced apart a slight bit farther leaving enough room to add the Leaf Green single lines. This will slightly change your coloring as well as give the plaid look instead of gingham checks. All these jumper segments will be shaded with a sideload float of Midnight Blue + a touch of Black.

5. BUTTONS ON SHIRT AND POCKET OF JUMPER: These are formed from either Creative Paperclay or Model Magic. Pinch off two tiny small amounts of clay and roll into smooth balls. Next, using a piece of wood, flatten these balls slightly to the desired size and diameter. Indent, leaving a rim around the outer edges. These are basecoated with Leaf Green and have Lt. Ivory crossing stitches in the center. Glue into place, one just under the chin on the upper shirt, and the other on the upper edge of the pocket on the jumper.

6. GARLAND AND STARS: The garland is made from some miniature greenery garland along with different sizes and shapes of wooden stars that have been painted and attached to decorate. I have taken two larger sized country quilt shaped stars and four smaller sized stars and basecoated them with Empire Gold. Doubleload highlight in the center of each star with Empire Gold and Crocus. Shade at each tip or point using a flat brush that has been loaded into extender and sideloaded into Mocha Brown. When dry, apply a heavy coat of Heavenly Hues Glitter. Attach the garland into each hand of the bear, securing with a touch of hot glue.

7. HALO: Shape with the gold craft wire and again secure with glue.

FINISH
Hot glue wings to back of bear. Varnish.

ANGEL WINGS

STAR CUTOUTS

LIL' ANGEL ADAM
COLOR PHOTO ON PAGE 57

This little boy angel is dedicated to the memory of one of God's "littlest angels." Adam will always stay tucked away in a corner of our family's hearts even though we never had the chance to know him, as he never had the opportunity to live, except for those special and precious minutes after his birth that passed for my lil' sis, her husband, and daughter. His existence will always be cherished. He's in God's hands now,...sittin' so proud on that puffy lil' cloud, holdin' on tight to his fishin' pole loaded with stars, showin' off to his daddy! 'Cause it's one of his dad's favorite pastimes to also hold a fishin' pole whenever he can get the time to.

Love to Adam, Lil' Sis, n' Family,

Aunt Debbie

PALETTE
DELTA CERAMCOAT
Black
Burnt Sienna
Cayenne
Crocus
Empire Gold
Flesh Tan
Ivory
Lt. Ivory
Maple Sugar Tan
Midnight Blue
Mocha Brown
Old Parchment
Spice Tan
DECOART AMERICANA
White Wash
DECOART HEAVENLY HUES
Glitter
ACCENT COUNTRY COLORS
Raw Sienna
JO SONJA'S ARTISTS' COLORS
Napthol Red Light
LIQUITEX TUBE ACRYLIC ARTIST COLORS
Burnt Umber

OTHER SUPPLIES
Black wire, double-braided
Craft buttons, 1 small tan, 1 baby red
Creative Paperclay
FolkArt Extender
Hot glue gun
Miniature silk poinsettias
Nylon fishing line
Split flower pot
Tacky Glue

WOOD SOURCE
Split flower pots and star cutouts may be purchased through:

Bear With Us, Inc.
8910 N. Greenhills Rd.
Kansas City, MO 64154-1501

PREPARATION
Sand, seal and sand again. Apply pattern for all basic design areas to be basecoated. (Re-apply pattern after the basecoating is completed to define all features, body sections, creases, folds, etc.)

PAINTING PROCEDURE
1. BEAR FUR: Basecoat with Spice Tan. Refer to the General Bear Instructions for the bear fur technique and specific palette that is used to complete the bear character.

2. GOWN: Basecoat the majority of the gown area, excluding the collar and cuffs, with Flesh Tan. Doubleload highlights with Flesh Tan and Ivory. Shade with a wider sideload float, first with Mocha, then deepen the shading using Burnt Umber. Spatter the gown with a fine mist of Burnt Umber.

3. COLLAR, TOE AREAS, HEEL, AND HEART PATCH: Basecoat with Napthol Red Light. Apply gingham checks using a liner brush. (Refer to the Terms And Techniques section for more instruction details for Painting Plaids And Checks.) NOTE: There is a slight portion of white showing on the bottom of the upper (back) foot, dividing the two feet. Shading and stitches for these areas and items are done with Black.

4. CUFFS, CENTER AREA ON SOCKS, AND SQUARE PATCH: Basecoat with Midnight Blue. The cuffs and socks are dry brushed with White Wash to give the denim look. (Refer to the Terms And Techniques section for more information and instruction on Dry Brushing.) Shade with a sideload float using Midnight Blue + a touch of Black. The stitches on the sleeves are Spice Tan. The patch will be made a plaid look using a liner brush and White Wash.

5. WINGS: Basecoat with Lt. Ivory and highlight using a doubleload of Lt. Ivory and White Wash. Sideload float shading with a mix of Midnight Blue + a touch of Black. Apply Heavenly Hues Glitter over the entire wing areas.

6. FLOWER POT: Basecoat with Cayenne and doubleload highlights using Cayenne and Ivory. Shade with a sideload float of Burnt Sienna. For Christmas time use, fill with poinsettias. For spring, change to miniature sunflowers. Glue the pot and flowers into place.

7. CLOUD: Apply different amounts of Creative Paperclay for a dimensional look. Build the clay heavier around the pot so it appears set in the clouds. (Refer to the Terms And Techniques section for more instruction on the use of Creative Paperclay and Model Magic.) Dry, sand, then basecoat with White Wash. There is very faint shading in some creases painted with Midnight Blue + a touch of Black. Apply Heavenly Hues Glitter.

8. HALO: The halo is formed from the black braided wire. Glue to secure.

9. CANE FISHING POLE: Using a dowel stick, apply a touch of Paperclay at each bamboo joint. Moisten the dowel, press on a ring of clay, then smooth. Dry. Basecoat with Maple Sugar Tan. Highlight with Ivory strokes throughout the pole. Shade first with Mocha Brown, then deepen the shading with Burnt Umber.

10. FISHING LINE: Using a length of nylon fishing line, connect loops to every other joint and also at the end of the dowel, where it will insert into the hole in the hand to mount. HINT: If you tie a knot in the line where it will glue to the joints on the pole, it will help allow the loops to flow where you want and when attaching to the pole it will give something to glue at each knot. I notched the tip end of the pole to slip the line through and glue. The remaining line should hang down below the pole to the level of the clouds. After completing the stars, use a thin line of Tacky Glue on the backs to attach the line to the stars.

11 STARS: Basecoat with Empire Gold and doubleload highlight with Empire Gold and Crocus. Shade using a sideload of Mocha Brown, then add the coverage of Heavenly Hues Glitter.

FINISH
Glue all pieces into place. Varnish.

©debbie mitchell '96

CUBBY COLLECTIONS
COLOR PHOTO ON FRONT COVER

PALETTE
DELTA CERAMCOAT
Black
Black Green
Bright Yellow
Burnt Sienna
Empire Gold
Flesh Tan
Hunter Green
Ivory
Leaf Green
Lt. Ivory
Maple Sugar Tan

Midnight Blue
Mocha Brown
Old Parchment
Pumpkin
Sandstone
Seminole Green
Spice Tan
Sunbright Yellow
Trail Tan
Yellow

DELTA CERAMCOAT GLEAMS
Kim Gold
DECOART AMERICANA
Dark Pine
Leaf Green
Mistletoe
Santa Red
Ultra Blue Deep
White Wash
ACCENT COUNTRY COLORS
Pineneedle Green
Raw Sienna
JO SONJA'S ARTISTS' COLORS
Napthol Red Light
LIQUITEX TUBE ACRYLIC ARTIST COLORS
Burnt Umber

OTHER SUPPLIES
Metallic gold tie cording, medium and fine
Miniature 3/4" tall icicles, approximately 5
Stylus
Tacky Glue

WOOD SOURCES
A large standard cheese box was used. It is 5" high and 13" in diameter. You may wish to have a larger, deeper size box. If so, enlarge your border width. Boxes are available from:

Designs by Bentwood, Inc.
170 Big Star Dr.
P.O. Box 1676,
Thomasville, GA 31792

PREPARATION
Sand, seal, and sand again. Apply the pattern for the basic design areas to be basecoated. Background areas, larger objects such as the window, half paneling, rug, packages, bears, desk, step ladder, etc. are examples of pattern items to trace at this time. It may be easier for you to do the wall, paneling, and floor areas first, then re-apply other parts of the pattern afterwards. Needless to say, there will be many pattern portions that will need individual applications, then painting before continuing. (As we have done in all other projects, re-applying patterns after each basecoating is completed will be required for defining features, body sections, creases, folds, frame work, shelves, and cabinet doors, etc.) You may wish to place the tree branches in after most everything surrounding that area of the box is completed. An example is, the shelf on the wall has branches that overlap. This will be up to you as to how much you prefer to have done and have to work around with the tree.

PAINTING PROCEDURE
1. UPPER WALL: Basecoat with Lt. Ivory, then using a large flat brush, load into extender and sideload into Ivory. Place a shadow along the left side of the corner line. Remaining shadows and shading will basically be behind several objects such as behind the right side of the desk, surrounding bodies of bears, edging close to the curtains, etc. This shade color may be using the Ivory first, then deepen with Raw Sienna very softly and faintly. Final shading to have a sharper, stronger shadow is with Burnt Umber. Some of the shadows that are cast in areas such as behind each of the candles, shaker boxes, and the sandstone crock are placed onto the wall by moistening the surface area with a satin film of extender. Brush back and forth in all directions until the surface is no longer dripping wet. Touch into Raw Sienna, work out to soften the color on the palette and place the shadow on the wall behind the object. Using a dry flat brush, lightly touch the surface to buff and soften the shadow, but be sure to keep it in the shape of the object that is casting the shadow.

2. PANELING: Basecoat with Hunter Green. Apply the pattern for the wood grooves and trims. Doubleload the highlights using Hunter Green and Lt. Ivory. Blend to soften the colors well on the palette. Follow the pattern and color photo for placement. Shade using a sideload float of Black Green. This shading will be to define the paneling details and the shadows under the window ledge, surrounding each bear that overlaps the green area, and underneath and along side edges of the desk. (NOTE: I actually ran my paneling all the way behind the tree to the corner of the wall. It creates a background behind the tree!)

3. FLOORING, WINDOW SILLS, DESK, AND DECORATIVE SHELF: Each have basically the same coloring. Wood stains can vary depending on your wood and paint used. I will be giving you a couple of combination options to try to get a look that will suit you individually.

OPTION #1: These particular segments that are listed above can be left open so that the natural wood of the box lid shows through. After the pattern for details is placed, then start shading with a sideload float of Burnt Umber. In the more open, larger areas such as those on the cabinet doors, it may require a wash of stain applied first before shading in the details. Upon completion of this shading, the object will then appear to have a complete stained look. If you were to stain with a wash of color in small areas, then shade, it may result in a really deep dark stain and the details may be difficult to see. We do want a stronger darker shadow underneath the rug and around the bears where they are up against the flooring. There should be deep and dark shadows that are deep inside the compartments of the desk, areas that form angles where shading needs to be deeper in color, and shadows that are cast from the desk cabinet onto the shelf edge will be examples of the strong shading that will need to be applied. All the sharp edges and lines that are defined have all been done with sideload floats using different sizes of brushes on the chisel edge.

OPTION #2: Similar looks can be also achieved by actually basecoating these wood areas with a tan base color then highlight with Old Parchment and possibly Ivory lightly in places. Shading will come in different layers, starting with a lighter color or possibly a medium brown color that has a touch of reddish cast to it. Then, deeper darker shading using Burnt Umber as discussed in the first option. An example of these color combinations then could be: Basecoat with something like Flesh Tan. Doubleload highlight with Flesh Tan and Old Parchment and possibly Ivory in some places. In the window, shelf, and desk the highlights and shading will be slightly yellow with a touch of reddish shading. Some combinations of shade colors can be done with a touch of Mocha Brown, then a bit of Burnt Sienna, then final deepening with Burnt Umber. When shading with the first colors, use extender on your brush instead of water when sideloading and blending colors. This will help keep the colors blended very softly. Be sure to add your knot holes and wood grain looks. The flooring will take on a little deeper brown stained look.

4. LADDER AND SPOOL CANDLE HOLDER ON SHELF: Basecoat with Flesh Tan and doubleload highlights with Flesh Tan and Ivory. Shade with Burnt Umber.

5. WINDOW: Basecoat inside the squares of the panes using Midnight Blue. With White Wash on a liner brush, basecoat the snow along the bottom ledges of each pane. Shading on the snow covered panes is sideload floated with Midnight Blue + a touch of Black. Sideload into White Wash and work on the palette well to soften, then streak a few diagonal lines in the centers of the blue square panes. These will appear to give a glass look. Sideload float shading surrounding the outer panes with Black. Spatter with White Wash using a toothbrush, leaving a very fine snow look outside.

6. CURTAIN SWAG: Basecoat with Napthol Red Light. Using a liner brush flattened when loading into a transparent amount of White Wash, apply the plaid look. (Refer to the Terms And Techniques section for more instructions on Painting Plaids And Checks.) Shade with a mixture of Napthol Red Light + a touch of Midnight Blue.

7. HEART BRACKETS TO HOLD UP CURTAIN SWAG: Mix a medium grey color using Black + White Wash. Load a liner brush and base in the heart shapes. With a small flat brush, sideload float with White Wash for some highlights, then shade with Black.

8. HEART WIRE CANDLE HANGER ON WALL AND SPIRAL WIRE CANDLE HOLDER ON DESK: Form with a liner brush and Black. Sideload lightly in some places with White Wash for highlights. The red tapered candles are basecoated with Napthol Red Light. The highlight is located in the center of each candle using a doubleload of Napthol Red Light and a touch of Pumpkin + Ivory. This will need to be completed before applying the spiral wire over the top.

9. SPOOL CANDLE HOLDER: Follow the instructions for the wooden look explained in Step #4. The upper and lower disc areas are basecoated with DecoArt Americana Leaf Green. Highlight with Mistletoe and shade with Black Green.

10. STACKABLE SHAKER BOXES: The lower box is basecoated with Midnight Blue and doubleload highlighted with Midnight Blue and White Wash. Shade with a mix of Midnight Blue + a touch of Black. The center box is basecoated with Santa Red and highlighted with a doubleload of Santa Red and Ivory. The shading is done with a mix of Santa Red + a touch of Midnight Blue. The upper box is basecoated with Hunter Green and doubleload highlighted with Hunter Green and Mistletoe. Shade with a sideload float of Black Green. The tiny brads on each box are dots of Kim Gold.

11. BASKET OF CINNAMON STICKS: Basecoat the basket with Trail Tan and highlight the weaves with a mix of Trail Tan + Ivory. Shading is done with Burnt Umber. Basecoat the cinnamon sticks with Burnt Sienna and highlight with Mocha Brown. Shading is done with a sideload float of Burnt Umber. Basecoat the ribbon with Napthol Red Light. Highlight with a touch of Napthol Red Light + a touch of Ivory or White Wash. Shade to distinguish the loops, knot, and streamers using a mix of Napthol Red Light + a touch of Midnight Blue.

12. HEARTS HANGING FROM PEGS: Basecoat with Napthol Red Light. Highlight with a doubleload of Napthol Red Light and White Wash. Shading is a mix of Napthol Red Light + Midnight Blue. The jute looking string connecting and hanging hearts from the pegs is done with any of your brown colors such as Trail Tan and a touch of Raw Sienna.

13. GREEN TAPERED CANDLES HANGING FROM SHAKER PEGS: Basecoat with DecoArt Americana Leaf Green and highlight in the centers with Mistletoe. Shade with a sideload float of Black Green along the left edge of each candle as well as the area where the bear ear overlaps the candles. The connecting wicks are Lt. Ivory or White Wash. Shade one chisel edge with Raw Sienna along the side of the wick itself.

14. THREE PUFFED HEARTS HANGING IN WINDOW: The two end hearts are basecoated with Mistletoe doubleloaded using White Wash. The left heart is dotted with Napthol Red Light print and the right heart is stripped with White Wash. Shade both hearts lightly along the left sides and a little up in the center crease with Black Green. The center heart is basecoated with White Wash and has tiny gingham checks done with a liner brush and Napthol Red Light. Shade with a mix of Napthol Red Light + a touch of Midnight Blue. The string and bows are basecoated with Trail Tan and detailed with Raw Sienna. Deepen the shading with Burnt Umber if needed.

(CONTINUED ON PAGE 52)

CUBBY COLLECTIONS
(CONTINUED FROM PAGE 51

15. THREE PINECONES ON TOP OF CABINET: Basecoat with Raw Sienna and highlight with Trail Tan. Shading is done with Burnt Umber.

16. CROCK ON TOP OF CABINET: Basecoat using Sandstone and highlight with a doubleload of Sandstone and Lt. Ivory. Shade with a mix of Sandstone + Black. You may wish to add a touch of Burnt Umber to the mix to muddy the grey look a bit. The strokes and trim colors are done with Midnight Blue and there is a Napthol Red Light Heart in the center of the crock.

17. RED AND GREEN PUFF HEART STRAND HANGING ON THE CABINET: There are a total of fifteen hearts alternately basecoated with Mistletoe and Napthol Red Light. Highlight the red hearts with a doubleload of Napthol Red Light and either White Wash or Ivory. Dot with tiny White Wash pindots. Shade with a mix of Napthol Red Light + a touch of Midnight Blue along the right side of each red heart and in the center creases. Highlight the green hearts with a doubleload of Mistletoe and White Wash. Shade with Black Green. (NOTE: In the beginning I planned to leave it at this point. Then, I continued to add a touch more blue to the piece by adding the beads and jingle bells.) Dot the beads between each heart with a mix of Ultra Blue Deep + White Wash. Shade the right side of each bead with Ultra Blue Deep and place a tiny White Wash highlight dot to the left upper side. The jingle bells are done with dots of Empire Gold. Highlight the left and lower edges using Ivory. Shade the upper edge with Mocha Brown. The opening slits are done with Burnt Umber. Shade around the hearts and bells, on the under side only, on the cabinet doors using Burnt Umber. There are Napthol Red Light streamers showing on the right side.

18. ITEMS ON DESK: The pen is basecoated with a lighter blue mix of Ultra Blue Deep + White Wash. Highlight with White Wash and shade with a chisel edge float along each side using Ultra Blue Deep. The ball point tip is painted with a grey mix of Black + White Wash. So is any highlights and shading on this tip. The cap on the back of the pen is Black. Then cast a shadow under the pen where it overlaps the edge of the shelf with Burnt Umber. Basecoat the post-it pad with White Wash, shade with Black and apply Ultra Blue Deep writing. Basecoat the candle tin with a medium grey mix of Black + White Wash. Highlight with White Wash and Shade with Black. The candle is painted the same as all of the others. Basecoat the stocking with White Wash for better coverage. Re-apply the pattern for the upper cuff, toe, and heel. Basecoat each of these areas with Napthol Red Light. Highlight with a doubleload of Napthol Red Light and Ivory. Shade with a mix of Napthol Red Light + Midnight Blue. There are two wider Napthol Red Light stripes and three Mistletoe stripes slightly more narrow. To give a rib knit look, shade the stripes throughout the stocking using Black.

19. RUG: The outer rings, three and four rows thick, are basecoated with Hunter Green. Repeat highlights and shading as we did with the paneling. Next are two rows of Lt. Ivory with Raw Sienna shading and details. Then we have two rows

basecoated with Santa Red and highlighted with a doubleload of Santa Red and Lt. Ivory. Shade with a mix of Santa Red + a touch of Midnight Blue. Add two more rows of Lt. Ivory, then use the Hunter Green again. Then you will see a small narrow space between the package and girl kneeling that will be Lt. Ivory, another Santa Red, then Lt. Ivory, and finally Hunter Green.

20. TWO PACKAGES UNDER TREE AND LADDER AREA: Basecoat with White Wash. The package on the left has gingham checks painted with a #1 flat brush and Napthol Red Light. The bow is Basecoated with Seminole Green and highlighted with Delta Ceramcoat Leaf Green. Shade the bow with Black Green. The box on the right has Mistletoe gingham checks with a Napthol Red Light heart pattern between. The ribbon around the box is Napthol Red Light, shaded with a mix of Napthol Red Light + Midnight Blue.

21. SPOOL OF RED RIBBONS AND ROLL OF WRAPPING PAPER AROUND THE BASE OF THE LADDER: Basecoat both spools and the roll of paper with White Wash. Stripe with the wrapping paper with horizontal stripes alternating with Napthol Red Light and Mistletoe. If there is any ribbon that is exposed it will be Napthol Red Light. All shading is done with a sideload float of Black.

22. LOOSE, PRE-FORMED BOW ON FLOOR TO LEFT OF ROOM AND SPOOL OF RIBBON TO RIGHT SIDE OF ROOM: The spool is painted the same as in step #21. The ribbons are basecoated with Ultra Blue Deep and doubleload highlighted with Ultra Blue Deep and White Wash. Shade with a mix of Ultra Blue Deep + a touch of Black.

23. LARGE PACKAGE IN CENTER OF RUG: Basecoat with Napthol Red Light and doubleload highlights using Napthol Red Light and Ivory or White Wash. Stripe with diagonal stripes of Ultra Blue Deep and Delta Ceramcoat Leaf Green. Shade with a mix of Napthol Red Light + Midnight Blue. The big ribbon and bow is basecoated with Seminole Green and doubleload highlighted with Delta Ceramcoat Leaf Green. To give a higher intensity add a touch of Bright Yellow. Shade with Black Green.

24. CHRISTMAS TREE: Start with the very basic, which will be a center trunk that will be thicker at the base and much more narrow at the top. Stem out with branches to start to form the tree shape. These all will be done with a thinned amount of Burnt Umber using a liner brush. Next, the branches and tree fullness will begin to form. Using a liner brush and Pineneedle Green, pull wispy strokes from the center of each branch and fill up the branch as you extend to the outer point. Gradually apply layers of colors getting lighter as you go. Pineneedle Green, Seminole Green, Leaf Green, and Bright Yellow will be the colors in sequence. I shaded with Black Green especially around the bodies of the bears.

25. MINIATURE LIGHTS: The wire and sockets are basecoated with Dark Pine and highlighted with a mix of Dark Pine + White Wash. Shade with Black Green. The light bulbs are basecoated with Napthol Red Light, Ultra Blue Deep, Pumpkin, Mistletoe, and Bright Yellow. Highlighting for each color can be achieved by using the base color and White Wash doubleloaded and blended well. Shading will be with the appropriate shade color as has been used in many other

objects. Shade the green bulbs lightly with Black Green. Shade the blue bulbs with Ultra Blue Deep. Shade the red bulbs with a mix of Napthol Red Light + a touch of Midnight Blue. Shade the orange bulbs with a mix of Pumpkin + a touch of Napthol Red Light. Shade the yellow bulbs with Yellow.

26. GINGERBEAR ORNAMENTS ON TREE: Basecoat with a mix of Spice Tan + a touch of Raw Sienna. Shade with a sideload float using Burnt Umber around the details such as the head, ears, and muzzles. The eyes and noses are Black with tiny dots of White Wash for highlights. The tongues, strings for hanging, and hearts in the tummies are Napthol Red Light. The icing on the arms and legs is White Wash. Shade on either side of this icing, at the scallops, using a sideload float of Burnt Umber

27. POPCORN AND CRANBERRY STRAND: Basecoat the popcorn with White Wash First. Using Spice Tan on a liner brush, apply the kernels somewhere inside an opening of the popcorn. Some may require a touch of Burnt Umber shading also. I do add a very slight touch of Sunbright Yellow washed over some of the pieces for a buttered effect. The cranberries may need a basecoat of White Wash first to have a better coverage. Then basecoat each berry with Napthol Red Light. Highlight with White Wash and shade with Napthol Red Light + a touch of Midnight Blue. You may require touching a bit of Black Green shading over the branches of the tree against the popcorn strand. This will help it stand out against the tree. OPTIONAL FEATURE: I took some of my tiny left-over icicles and glued into place as added decorations on the tree.

28. GREENERY ALONG TOP OF CABINET: This will be the same technique and colors as the tree branches. Once all the objects are completed on top, place the greenery in and around them.

29. BEAR FUR TECHNIQUE: Basecoat with Spice Tan. Refer to the General Bear Instructions for the bear fur technique and the specific palette that is used to complete the bear characters.

30. BOY BEAR KNEELING AT PACKAGE: Basecoat the gown, toes, and heel with Napthol Red Light. Highlight with a doubleload of Napthol Red Light and Pumpkin + a touch of Ivory. Shade with a mix of Napthol Red Light + Midnight Blue. Basecoat the socks, neck, sleeve, and gown trims all with White Wash. Stripe the socks with Napthol Red Light. Shading on these areas is painted with a sideload float of Black. There are Black stitches along the toes and heel.

31. GIRL BEAR KNEELING AT PACKAGE: Basecoat the gown with Seminole Green and doubleload highlight with Seminole Green and Delta Ceramcoat Leaf Green, adding a touch of Bright Yellow if needed. Stripe the gown with the highlight color. Between each stripe is a cluster of four White Wash dots and between these is a tiny Napthol Red Light heart. Shade with Black Green. The sleeve and collar ruffle and gown ruffle are basecoated with White Wash and shaded with Black + a touch of Midnight Blue. The hair bow and slippers are basecoated with Napthol Red Light and doubleload highlighted with Napthol Red Light and Pumpkin + a touch of Ivory. Shade with a mix of Napthol Red Light + Midnight Blue.

32. BEAR HOLDING WRAPPING PAPER: Basecoat the pajamas using Napthol Red Light. Stripe using White Wash, then shade with a mix of Napthol Red Light + Midnight Blue. The cardboard area of the ribbon roll in her hands is basecoated with White Wash and trimmed with Mistletoe, then shaded with Black. The ribbon streamer is basecoated with Mistletoe and doubleload highlighted with White Wash. Shade with Black Green. The green wrapping is painted in the same color combinations as the ribbon streamer with the exception that the paper is dotted with White Wash. Basecoat the other two rolls with White Wash first. One is striped with larger Napthol Red Light lines with thin double lines of Mistletoe between. The last roll is lined with plaid using Napthol Red Light. Shade with Black Green. Basecoat the scissors handles with Black and highlight lightly using White Wash. The remaining scissors portion is basecoated with a mix of Black + White Wash for a grey color. Shade with Black and highlight with White Wash.

33. BEAR ON LADDER: Basecoat the pajamas with a mix of Ultra Blue Deep + White Wash. Doubleload highlights using this mix and a touch more White Wash on one side of the brush. Shade using a sideload float of Ultra Blue Deep adding a touch of Black if necessary. The elbow and knee pads and back flap are basecoated with White Wash. Apply a gingham check pattern using a liner brush and Napthol Red Light. The popcorn strand described in Step #29 is continued down across the body of the bear and the step ladder. You will need to paint this section after the bear clothing and ladder are completed.

34. BEAR CARRYING PACKAGES: Basecoat the lower dress, hat, and center package with Napthol Red Light and doubleload highlights using Napthol Red Light and Pumpkin + Ivory. The hat and lower dress have a print pattern of four cluster dots of White Wash. Shade with a mix of Napthol Red Light + a touch of Midnight Blue. The ruffle on the hat is White Wash, shaded with a mix of Midnight Blue + a touch of Black. The upper dress or apron is basecoated with DecoArt Americana Leaf Green and doubleload highlighted with Leaf Green and Mistletoe. Shade with Black Green. Sideload the tip of a small flat brush into White Wash, then apply C-strokes across the bottom of the apron to look like lace. The upper package is basecoated with Lt. Ivory and has Mistletoe gingham checks. Shade using Black Green. The lower package is painted the same as the red plaid wrapping paper described in Step #32.

35. BEAR ON SHOULDERS: Basecoat the pajamas with Napthol Red Light and doubleload highlight with Napthol Red Light and Pumpkin + a touch of Ivory. The collar, button flap, and dots in shirt are White Wash. There are Napthol Red Light heart buttons on the flap. Shade with a mix of Napthol Red Light + a touch of Midnight Blue. The star in her hand is basecoated with Empire Gold and doubleload highlighted with Empire Gold and Sunbright Yellow. Shade first with Mocha, then deepen the shading if necessary with Burnt Umber. Place a Napthol Red Light heart in the center of the star.

53

(CONTINUED ON PAGE54)

(CONTINUED FROM PAGE 53)

36. BEAR IN SHORTS: Basecoat the portion of T-shirt with a grey mix of Black + White Wash. Highlight using a doubleload of the grey mix and White Wash. Shade with a deeper grey tone. The shorts are basecoated with Ultra Blue Deep and doubleload highlighted with Ultra Blue Deep and White Wash. Shade with a mix of Ultra Blue Deep + a touch of Black to deepen the color. The buttons at the waist are Napthol Red Light with Ultra Blue Deep stitches. The bear is standing on a foot stool that is very hard to see. So hard, that I almost missed it in these directions! Do as we did the step ladder.

37. BORDER AROUND THE OUTER EDGE OF LID: Measure off a 1 1/4" wide band all the way around the lid to form your border area. Basecoat this area and continue down the sides using Hunter Green. I like transferring my patterns on dark background colors either with a grey chalk pencil or white graphite paper. Transfer the pattern for the lights and ribbon. Basecoat the ribbon with Napthol Red Light and doubleload highlights with Napthol Red Light and Pumpkin + a touch of Ivory. Shade with a mix of Napthol Red Light + a touch of Midnight Blue.

38. LIGHT STRAND: The wire and bulb sockets are basecoated with Dark Pine and highlighted with a doubleload of Dark Pine and White Wash, blended well. Shade with Black Green. Beginning at the very top of the border pattern under the knot of the bow and working clockwise basecoat the bulbs in sequence using Mistletoe, Pumpkin, Napthol Red Light, Bright Yellow, and Ultra Blue Deep. Repeat the sequence around the entire border. Refer to the instructions for painting the light strand on the Christmas tree in Step #25 for information as to how to highlight and shade the lights. The colors will be the same. Shade using Black Green around portions of each light bulb on the Hunter Green surface to help the bulbs stand out stronger.

39. LOWER PORTION OF THE BOX SIDES: Basecoat with Napthol Red Light. Using a stylus and White Wash, apply a dot print. I measured and marked the staggered dot print using my grey chalk pencil and spaced the dots 1" apart before applying paint.

40. INSIDE LID AND INSIDE OF BOX: Basecoat with Hunter Green.

FINISH

Glue the gold metallic tie cording into place around the border. The very thin cord is placed at the inside edge of the border and the heavier cording is placed along the outer edge. Varnish inside and outside. Use several coats for protection.

BOTTOM LEFT
BORDER MOTIF

BOTTOM RIGHT
BORDER MOTIF

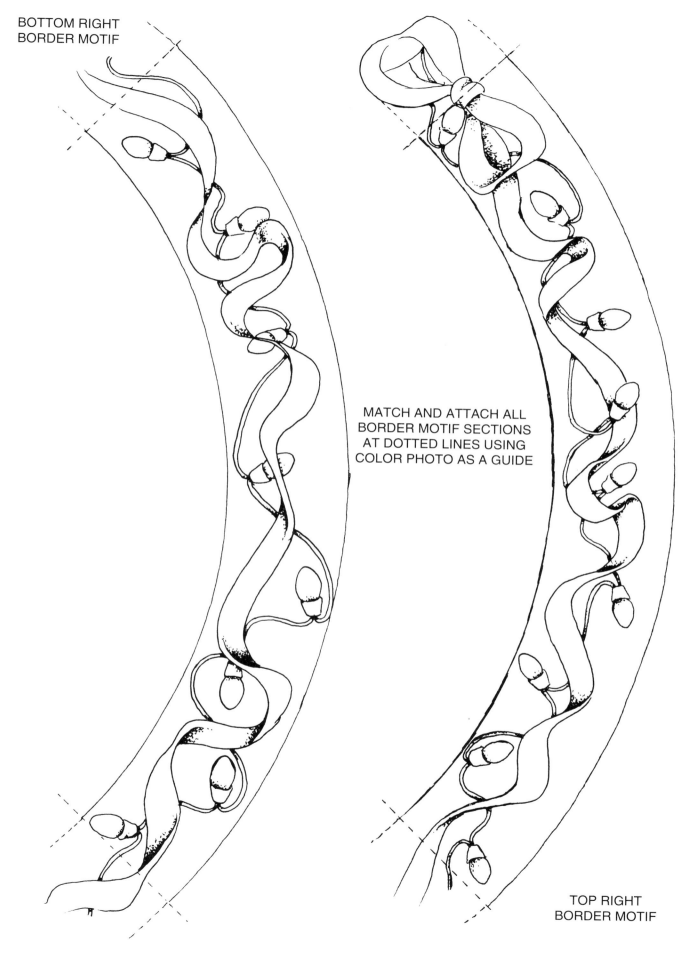

MATCH AND ATTACH ALL
BORDER MOTIF SECTIONS
AT DOTTED LINES USING
COLOR PHOTO AS A GUIDE

TOP RIGHT
BORDER MOTIF

CUBBY COLLECTIONS

CENTER BOX TOP MOTIF
MAIN SECTION
MATCH AND ATTACH WITH REMAINING
PATTERN SECTION ON PAGE 58
INSTRUCTIONS ON PAGES 50 THRU 54

©debbie mitchell '96

FOOTLOOSE N' HEAVENLY
Pages 46 and 47

GINGERBREAD GOODIES
Pages 43 thru 45

Cubby Collections
CENTER BOX TOP MOTIF

RIGHT SECTION

MATCH AND ATTACH WITH MAIN PATTERN
SECTION ON PAGE 56

INSTRUCTIONS ON PAGES 50 THRU 54